Mind Tricks
Our brain is the limit.
Cognitive processes in
Sign Language Interpreting

Proceedings of the 22nd efsli Conference
Antwerp, Belgium, 12th -14th September 2014

Edited by
Sarah Bown
Kristiaan Dekesel
Christopher Stone

ISBN 9789081306584
© European Forum of Sign Language Interpreters, 2015
Edited by: Sarah Bown, Kristiaan Dekesel & Christopher Stone
Cover design: Triin Jõeveer
Cover photos: BVGT and Lourdes Calle-Alberdi
Printed by: *Createspace*

This publication is made possible with the support of the Erasmus Plus Programme. The European Commission support for the production of this publication does not constitute an endorsement of the contents which reflects the views only of the authors, and the Commission cannot be held responsible for any use which may be made of the information contained therein

All rights reserved
No part of this publication may be produced, stored in a retrieval system or transmitted in any form or any means (electronic, photocopying, recording or otherwise), without the prior written permission of the publisher.

Table of contents

Foreword by Christian Peters, efsli President 4

Foreword by Debra Russell, WASLI president 6

"Shared mind – shared effort": the cognitive processes and strategies applied by trainee sign language interpreters 12
Sarah Bown and Kristiaan Dekesel

Sign Language Interpreting, challenges, tactics and efforts 48
Sophie Pointurier-Pournin

"Oil on troubled waters": a metaphorical perspective on interpreting and politeness 63
Rachel Mapson

Interpreting concerts 82
Rafaela Cota Silva

Abstracts of the conference 101

About the conference presenters 118

FOREWORD

Christian Peters

The efsli conference 2014 was held in Antwerp, Belgium from the 12th to the 14th September 2014, and was hosted by the Belgian Flemish Sign Interpreter Association, BVGT. The theme of the conference was 'Mind Tricks' - a theme that is always important for the interpreter's regular work. The conference provided an opportunity to bring together good practice and research findings on the cognitive processes that occur during simultaneous (sign language) interpreting. We sign language interpreters are always challenged when interpreting across different modalities- the spoken/written language modality and the sign language modality - and as they are so different, we always need 'Mind Tricks' for this work, helping us to juggle spoken, written and signed texts. We all shared our tricks for providing the best possible work as professional service providers, and in the process, widened our perspectives on our working processes. This made the conference just as special as every efsli conference we have had in the past.

The conference was a success, as can be seen just from the number of attendees. More than 230 participants from all over Europe came to Antwerp to learn about Mind Tricks, and share their tricks with each other, over the course of 10 brilliant presentations. The president of the World Association of Sign Language Interpreters (WASLI), Debra Russell from Canada, joined us as a keynote speaker with the theme "Consecutive and Simultaneous Interpreting: Research, Reality and Reflection". At the General Assembly, efsli's annual gathering before the conference, Debra signed a new Memorandum of Understanding with our former president Peter Llewellyn-Jones. This will strengthen cooperation between efsli and WASLI, who will meet to share achievements, developments, initiate new projects together and support each other.

I would like to express my sincere thanks to all presenters and participants for joining us in Antwerp for this fantastic conference, which was made successful by the BVGT organizing committee and their volunteers. On behalf of the efsli board I also want to thank them, for giving us the opportunity to learn so much - and giving us a bag full of Mind Tricks to bring home!

Christian Peters
efsli President

FOREWORD

Debra Russell

Dear colleagues:

The 2014 efsli conference in Antwerp, Belgium addressed the important theme of the cognitive processes that interpreters use on a daily basis in order to perform their work effectively. These "mind tricks" were illuminated across the range of conference presentations, delivered by interpreters, interpreter researchers and interpreters educators from Austria, Belgium, Canada, France, Ireland, Norway, Portugal, the United Kingdom, and the United States. Our sincere thanks to the conference organizers for creating such an outstanding program that brought together a great deal of current research and practice, and to each of the presenters for their generous contribution to these proceedings. While reading the proceedings doesn't give the reader a sense of the energy and excitement displayed by conference delegates as they engaged in discussion and debate about the ideas, is does offer you a glimpse of the range of evidence about the cognitive processes and decisions that shape our practice.

The program was varied and stimulating, and while not all of the presenters have been able to contribute to this volume, I have taken the liberty to describe what they offered to the conference delegates, so that you might get a taste of their fine work and seek out their publications.

Across the summaries compiled in this proceeding, you will see a number of connections, beginning by exploring the evidence about consecutive interpreting (CI) and simultaneous interpreting (SI) in two areas of our work – legal and educational setting. The nature of the evidence invites us to consider all of the tools we need in our satchel of mind tricks - CI/SI techniques, especially in one-to-one discourse events that are framed by medical, legal and employment discourse. This research emphasizes that translation, focused on the functionality of the discourse, combined with the cultural knowledge of working with Deaf people, underpins all effective interpretation. When we focus on the pragmatic and functionality of the discourse, there are opportunities to lessen the *illusion of inclusion*, i.e. the appearance of sign language being used that does not allow for meaningful communication access. One of the positive consequences in an educational setting is that meaning-based interpreting can allow for active engagement vs. creating a context where the Deaf child becomes a passive learner, or a bystander in the classroom of hearing children (Russell, 2002, 2005, 2008; Russell & Winston, 2014).

Sarah Bown and Kristiaan Dekesel (Belgium) offered an example of the use of Think Aloud Protocols (TAP) research in our field raising the question of how can we teach people to think more critically about their work and how we can help learners to do better by accessing their thought processes, adopting TAPs as a methodology.

Terry Janzen and Barbara Shaffer (Canada/US) engaged us in a thought-provoking discussion of intersubjectivity in communication, something each of us experience while engaged in communication. Their work helps us to examine how interpreters may structure their discourse-based decisions on perceptions and contextualization strategies. We facilitate that intersubjectivity based on our perceptions of the relationship between communicators. A key question these authors asked us to reflect upon from a cognitive linguistic perspective is "Where is meaning found?".

Christopher Stone and David Vinson (UK/US) shared their work on aptitude testing with BSL interpreters in order to address the question whether we can identify who is most suited to successful sign language interpreting. Their studies explored whether psychomotor speed increases with experience and their findings show that professional interpreters do not improve their psychomotor speed after training; while task switching and conflict process appear to improve based on BSL, leading us to understand that we must use specific training or development to better what interpreters do.

Sophie Pointureir-Pourin (France) provided an excellent overview of the challenges for signed language interpreters by examining our work through a transposition of the Gile Effort Model of interpreting. Her work reveals that discourse analysis is not an automatic effort process and that interpreter's attentional resources are limited, and crucially needed for interpreting.

Anna-Lena Nilsson (Norway) shared her research on the use of signing space and how interpreters mark the discourse on the body. Her research focused on experienced L1 and L2 users of Swedish Sign Language and her results demonstrate that L1 interpreters use three movement patterns in order to effectively mark discourse. This has important implications for teaching interpreters.

Lorraine Leeson (Ireland), Beppie van den Bogaerde (Netherlands) and Myriam Vermeerbergen (Belgium) conducted comparisons of Deaf clients' strategies for working with sign language interpreters and their criteria for selecting an interpreter and how they assess the competencies of the interpreters and strategies to work with interpreters. Their findings stress the concept of 'attitude' as key to building trust between Deaf consumers and interpreters, which includes accepting feedback from Deaf people about the interpreter's performance.

Rachel Mapson (United Kingdom) studied metaphor use in BSL and English, by looking at how interpreters recognize politeness in BSL and reflect that in English construction. Her findings show that interpreters can convey metaphors through six non-manual features and these devices are tied to relationship building and power. When we think about the important roles Deaf people play in daily life, meeting with non-deaf people, and how we represent Deaf people across a range of settings with a variety of social norms, the importance of our work is illuminated.

Lorraine Leeson and Casey Ferrara's (Ireland) described their work on the project known as *Irish President for All* highlighted identity marking and code switching in Irish and English. Their findings point to the coping strategies interpreter's use for dealing with two languages within an interpreted interaction and saving face.

Finally, Rafaela Cota Silva (Portugal) presented a music translation project using Portuguese Sign Language. Her work emphasizes the role of preparation in translation of artistic works, and in essence, offered us examples that touched on the themes within each of our presentations.

As we reflect on "mind tricks", it is clear that there is much to learn from the scholarship that shapes effective interpreting practice, from understanding and applying the translation/CI/SI continuum in our daily interpreting decisions, to recognizing intersubjectivity in the co-construction of interpreted discourse, leading us to examine the ways in which we represent identity. Exploring what L1 signers do with their linguistic knowledge of space provides us with strategies, both as interpreters and educators, to take to our life-long language learning. As our profession examines the pragmatic and functionality of language, in addition to the discourse, grammar and lexicon, we will witness a shift in our teaching and interpreting practice. Mind tricks, as a phrase applied to interpreting, requires us to articulate our strategies and mental models to extend our understanding of the complexity of our work. The use of TAPs is a tool that can be used to identify our cognitive processing challenges, including the interpreter's knowledge of language and culture. Our attention of pragmatics and functionality in the broadest sense also requires us to think about the audience for whom we construct our interpretation, whether that be the Deaf child in a classroom, the Deaf witness in a courtroom, the Deaf politician meeting with constituents, or Deaf community members attending a music festival. Our presence in each interpreted interaction places us in position of privilege and power, which requires us to know our own minds very well, in order to make reasoned and appropriate decisions in the many contexts in which we work.

Around the world, human rights and Deaf people is a central theme. Deaf people are participating in all aspects of life. Our conference presentations have demonstrated the many ways the interpreters are a key piece of supporting human rights for Deaf people – and if we are to do this well, we must keep learning, and that is what efsli has offered each of us.

Thank you to efsli and the BVGT Scientific Committee for preparing such an interesting conference. We hope that these proceedings accomplish what the conference did - keeping us talking, questioning, and thinking for many days to come.

Happy reading,
Debra Russell
WASLI President

"Shared mind – shared effort": the cognitive processes and strategies applied by trainee sign language interpreters.

Sarah Bown
Kristiaan Dekesel
University of Wolverhampton, UK
s.bown@wlv.ac.uk
k.dekesel@wlv.ac.uk

1. **Introduction**

As interpreter educators we often inform our trainees that there are multiple ways of doing things in order to achieve an effective interpretation. Bellos confirms that

> "... One of the most awkward & wonderful truths about translation... Any utterance of more than trivial length has no one translation. All utterances have innumerably many acceptable translations." (2011:5)

The early needs of trainee sign language interpreters, however, often results in an insistence of being shown the 'right' way or being provided with 'show and tell' concrete examples (modelling). It is also the case that trainees are often understandably intrigued by what their peers, and in particular what other qualified interpreters, might actually do in the situation they are presented with. Their view of translation is that educators will provide them with recipes to follow, indicating the exact ingredients, whereas the reality is that they are eventually required as interpreting professionals, to be able to cook without recipes.

Though trainees are provided with a range of models, approaches, procedures and strategies, their personal selection from those available, in other words which they apply or do not apply, is not always obvious in their end product. There is an understandable obsession from various stakeholders towards this end product created by interpreters, especially given that a tangible error analysis , for example Cokely (1986; 1992), can be conducted to indicate the so called 'flaws'. From an educational and developmental perspective, however, we are more interested in the choices that lead to this product, namely the process. We are of the view that overall quality can be enhanced by "manipulating" or "tinkering" with the thoughts behind the choices made (Bown & Dekesel, 2011, 2012), in order to achieve the ultimate goal which Nord defines as "*what should be going on in a translator's mind*" (1991:234).

Interpreter educators have long been fascinated by the interpreter's mind, but an interpreter's thought processes are not easily extracted, as these can only be retrieved by embarking on a process oriented approach. In their attempts to access the 'black box' (make the invisible visible) researchers utilised Ericsson & Simon's 1984 *think aloud protocols* (Krings, 1986; Tirkkonen-Condit & Jääskeläinen,

2000) based upon the agreed realisation that access to this box "*could afford exciting insights*" (Anderson, 1994:118).

This paper explores the documenting of trainee interpreters' thought processes, via the use of an on-line forum *Wolverhampton Online Learning Framework* (WOLF, first available at the University of Wolverhampton in 1996) and seeks to answer three questions:

1. What are the regularly occurring thoughts of trainee sign language interpreters; do they reveal the 'strategies' employed, and can a taxonomy be established from this?

2. Could the insight gained by the predominance, or absence, of certain thought processes inform a specific personal development plan for a trainee?

In other words, can thought processes identify issues with: language proficiency, comprehension of source language text, lack of knowledge of the range of strategies available, ongoing questions and decisions about their role boundaries, continuing professional development requirements and fitness to practice concerns.

3. Is there evidence that a *collective mind approach* (described below) benefits the development of interpreters?

Vygotsky (1978) argues for the establishment of a social learning community, to support an individual's learning and lead to the enhancement of the co-construction of knowledge.

Via access to the cognitive processes of their peers and the opportunity to provide/receive feedback, the collective mind approach has also been designed to promote co-learning and eventual co-working in professional life. The end aim was to equip both trainee and professional interpreters with a diagnostic tool to visualise their own thoughts, be exposed to alternative strategies employed by others, and to help them evaluate their developmental needs.

2. Un-tapping potential: From TAPs to WAPs

In 1984, Ericsson and Simon published their work entitled: 'protocol analysis' in which they discussed the assumptions, techniques and limitations, of exploring cognitive processes via the use of a subject's own verbal reports as data. This 'thinking aloud' approach was also utilised in the field of engineering to overcome problems by having individuals verbalise their thoughts, so others could easily and immediately access their train of thought. It did not take long before this 'think aloud protocol' was adopted by researchers in the field of spoken language translation and interpreting, in their quest to access the black box within a practitioner's mind (Krings 1986, 1987; Séguinot 1996; Tirkkonen-Condit and Jääskeläinen 2000; Bernardini 2001; Jääskeläinen 2002; Li 2004) and subsequently also in the field of sign language interpreting (Stone 2007; Bown and Dekesel 2011, 2012; Smith 2014; Russell and Winston 2014).

In this study, the 'think aloud protocols' (TAPs) were adjusted to a written format or 'write aloud protocols' (WAPs) to document the thought processes of trainee sign language interpreters during the task of translating a text from English to British Sign Language (BSL), (see appendix). This was facilitated by the use of 'track changes' within Microsoft Word software, which allowed individuals to pinpoint the verbalisation of their thoughts to specific passages in the text under consideration.

As educators, we were therefore able to identify which parts of the text sparked off a particular thought process and *"The use of TAPs, and the subsequent analysis into thought categories, allowed us as trainers to directly intervene by identifying areas of development"* (Bown & Dekesel, 2012:31).

3. **Shared mind = shared effort**

The interpreting: (BSL/English) degree programme at the University of Wolverhampton has incorporated on-line learning, since 1996, as part of its blended learning strategy to accompany the face to face delivery of training. Though Tiene (2000) has found that students prefer face-to-face rather than online engagement when both are available, and many regard e-learning as an addition to live discussion, the benefits of e-learning are numerous. E-learning, has the learner as its central focus (Zhang, Zhao, Zhou, &

Nunamaker, 2004), it has the option to preserve anonymity (Roffe, 2002), it affords the potential of group collaboration and teamwork (Capper, 2001; Thurmond et al., 2002), it allows for synchronous and asynchronous interaction (Keegan, 2000), increases opportunity for formative assessment and feedback (JISC, 2008), it improves the process of knowledge acquisition (Radović-Marković, 2010), and can identify learning styles (Salmon, 2006). It was therefore regarded as an ideal vehicle for the purposes of this study, i.e. the documenting of the thought processes of trainee sign language interpreters and the sharing of these thoughts with others.

Within the WOLF virtual learning environment, we set up a 'collective mind', to which all trainees within a cohort contribute. The collective mind consists of four set components produced by each individual trainee, namely: a skills gap analysis, an English/BSL glossary, a write aloud protocol document and a signed translation (end product). This is accompanied by an end product example translation from a professional translator, which is only released after each trainee had uploaded their own contributions and taken part in a range of collaborative tasks involving accessing the minds of other individuals.

The skills gap analysis, consist of a pre-determined group of questions which function as a framework to identify the demands of a translation assignment. It questions whether the trainee has the necessary skills to undertake the task required and whether any shortcomings can be overcome.

It links directly into the UK national occupational standards of interpreters (CiLT, 2006, 2010), which requires that interpreters establish the nature of assignments and whether they have the right skills.

The trainee's English to BSL glossary establishes their comprehension of concepts. The efforts of an individual contribute to a collective glossary and identify multiple strategies. This approach is supported by AIIC (2013) who advocate that *""It can be very helpful to cross-reference your glossary against those prepared by other colleagues... you may find that there are other translations for terms that you have already captured"*. The glossary English to BSL provides suitable BSL translations, in particular where an established BSL translation cannot easily be identified.

The write aloud protocols highlight where the mind pauses to overcome challenges within the text and sheds light on the strategies employed to overcome them. The exact moment when a trainee pauses are indicated by where the track changes occur. Though individual trainees may have misgivings about their own shortcomings, as to where their mind stumbles, and at times cannot find a wholly satisfactory solution to a problem, they do find reassurance when looking into the WAPs of others and find that similar issues have been identified. As a collective, however, they learn from the choices and decisions made by their peers and are quick to identify the most favourable strategies.

The interpreter trainees' BSL end product is used for a range of collaborative activities (pair and group). The signed clips are glossed and evaluated for strengths and areas for development. The outcomes are then cross referenced with individual WAPs and glossaries, in order to find the thought processes behind the decisions made. With this evidence to hand and access to the 'collective mind', alternative strategies are then explored, via group discussion, facilitated by interpreter educators.

The professional example is used by the trainees to undertake a comparative analysis, via Sampaio's (2007) evaluation criteria, with their own end product. They identify and discuss contrasting translation approaches/strategies and attempt to deconstruct the thought processes behind the decisions in the end product of the professional translator. In the end, rather than wanting the 'one way' to solve a challenge, the trainees come to the realization that *"A major source of variability in the individual translating is the number of strategies available for performing the task"* Séguinot (1997:109).

4. The research: the thoughts of trainee interpreters

In order to arrive at a suitable taxonomy of trainee interpreter's thoughts, one would need to systematically classify or establish an ordered arrangement of all the thoughts that occurred within our online 'collective mind'. Many taxonomies have been proposed in the past, though Avval's review of taxonomies suggests that *"Over the years, there have been about nine key taxonomies..."* (2012:768). Alongside these key taxonomies, the conceptual maps constructed by Van Doorslaer in 2007, which focus on the possible translation approaches, strategies and procedures that form part of a translator's repertoire, and the research carried out by Shirvani (2009) into learning strategies employed during translation, also provide a useful guide as to the creation of a translation taxonomy.

Practitioners in the field of sign languages, however, may be more familiar with Cokely's miscue analysis taxonomy (1986, 1992), where the focus is, amongst other factors, on omissions, additions and anomalies in the end product. When looking at the research into translation/interpreting we find an extensive range of studies based on an analysis of 'end product evidence'; the sign language studies which focus on 'in process evidence', for example by means of TAPs, are unfortunately not that extensive, even though one could argue this type of research would play a crucial role in the pedagogic developmental of interpreters. Russell and Winston assert that 'in process evidence' has the potential to *"...reveal the strategies interpreters use to solve interpretation challenges..."* (2014:120).

Some of the recent studies which utilise TAPs/WAPs to gather evidence of an interpreter's thought processes, have each come up with classification suggestions in order to categorise the thoughts collected. In our research on interpreter thoughts during sight translation, we constructed the following classification: domain knowledge

& specifics, audience, vocabulary, syntax, time and quality boundaries, comprehension, re-structure and equivalence, justifications & implications, legal issues, creativity (Bown & Dekesel, 2011, 2012). Other studies have grouped thoughts together around 'intent, audience, role and sign choices' (Russell & Winston, 2014) and recently Smith (2014) classified thoughts into: 'models employed, ethical reasoning and vocabulary range'.

Though thought processes, and hence classification categories, may vary in their predominance depending on situational factors, mode of translation/interpretation, an interpreter's experience, nature of texts used, to mention but a few, certain thought processes and therefore categories such as, 'audience', 'restructure', 'role', 'risk' and 'glossary', one would expect to occur in any occasion/assignment, and our current study is no exception. When classifying thoughts into categories, certain thoughts could easily fit into more than one category, and although we established an extensive range of thought categories within our taxonomy, for the purposes of this study we will only focus on: risk, role, audience, rhetorical questions and glossary. For ease of identification, the thoughts of the trainee interpreters taking part in this research study, will be represented by using square brackets.

The trainee interpreters who participated in this study, were undertaking level 5 of their training programme, which is either the 2nd or 3rd year of their course, dependent upon the point of entry. At this point they are about to complete the intermediate British Sign Language and consecutive interpreting modules. The trainee interpreters were presented with a short text (see appendix) which was widely available in the public domain and contained information about 'Voting for the Mayor of London' and was accompanied by a translation 'brief'. They were informed that the end product was going to be published on the web. The primary audience, therefore, would be potential voters in the London area, but could theoretically be viewed by anyone throughout the country.

4.1 Risk

The National Registers of Communication Professionals working with Deaf and Deafblind People (NRCPD), the professional registration body of interpreters states in their code of conduct for communication professionals (2010), which all registered interpreters must adhere to, that as an interpreter " *you must recognise and work within the limits of your competence, and if necessary, refer on to another proficient professional"* and that *"You should only undertake assignments for which you have the appropriate qualifications, competence, and experience"*. The trainees were required when analysing the text to assess the level of 'risk' involved. This included evaluating its level of importance and the implications of undertaking the assignment for themselves and their clients.

A point for perennial discussion is: how do interpreters assess and assign risk? Determining the level of risk, involves a coming together of a number of factors, for example, situational variables/protocols , topic knowledge/terminology, domain preference/anxiety, language proficiency (spoken and signed language) and an interpreter's level of training undertaken to date.

The thought processes revealed a range of views, at times divergent:

> *[There is a risk but it is **not overly high**]*
> *[There are **some elements** which are **less vital**]*

The trainees personal views on the voting process, their voting experiences and whether voting was seen as a democratic right impacted on the level of risk perceived, given that who you vote for can affect your daily life:

> *[this is a **very critical** piece of information...it is **high risk** because they have **a right** to access information]*
> *[The content of the text is **important political information**]*

Risk was also determined by assessing whether harm would or could be caused to Deaf clients:

> *[The impact of the source text meaning being lost is **not life threatening** but it is **a right**]*
> *[a misunderstanding would **not result in a life or death situation**... not receiving the info **may cause problems** for prospective voters]*

> [Document **not high risk** as to not have this information on how to vote would **not be detrimental** to the Deaf person's well-being.]

In some instances, risk was assessed via the perspective of the translator only, through assumptions made about the text density, complexity and familiarity.

> [text difficulty = **low risk**]

4.2 Role

At this stage of their development, the trainee interpreters are exploring and shaping the concept of 'role'. This is by its very nature multifaceted and has a myriad of boundaries. To date, they have been exposed to historical and current thinking about an interpreter's role from the viewpoint of interpreter educators, client expectations, professional bodies, practitioners and professional membership organisations. The latter often provide guidelines for interpreting in specific settings (education, health, access to work), as is the case for the Association of Sign Language Interpreters (ASLI) in the UK. The notion of role, however, is constantly being challenged and redefined, as evidenced by a recent example from Llewellyn-Jones & Lee's (2014) 'role-space model', in which they argue that *"...interpreters need, above else, to be 'rounded' human beings with well-honed social skills, sensitivities and awareness, as well as having excellent linguistic skills."* (p. 148)

By examining the trainee interpreters' thought processes, we ascertain they are aware that there are role boundaries that require adherence to:

> *[I might be tempted to go into **too much detail**, as to be **fully inclusive**. However, I must be careful to **not overstep the line**]*

Some consider that their role may at times include being an educator, based on their growing awareness of the diversity of educational opportunities and subsequent attainment within the Deaf community to which they have been exposed:

> *[possibly have to **become an educator** to explain... this could be seen as a **role boundary issue**]*
> *[there are not yet any known role boundary issues... it is **all quite self-explanatory**]*

There are some, though, that question how far they adopt this educator role, given their rather literal interpretation of the NRCPD's Code of Conduct for Communication Professionals (2010) which states that "...you should not add nor take anything away from the intended meaning and should keep to the spirit of what is said or signed."

> *[should include **little 'education'** and rather be a translation]*

This can create an extreme view by setting the educator role beyond the boundaries of the interpreter and putting the responsibility for the acquisition of knowledge firmly back on the Deaf clients:

> *[anyone who requires further info on this can **go and research it themselves**]*

Closely linked to the role of educator are those that see it as their remit to facilitate comprehension, taking into account the linguistic variety demonstrated by the Deaf community:

> *[I shall **back up information** just in case]*
> *[**reinforcement** of some content to ensure as many people as possible understand]*

Some thoughts could be seen as a possible cause for concern or as evidence that, even at the trainee stage, an interpreter's role is not perceived as fixed. Instead the need to be flexible, in order to accommodate different situations/assignments, has been identified, and that one should avoid a limited or narrow view when setting role boundaries, given that an interpreter may be required to adjust their role even within a single assignment:

> *[role boundary issues - **none identified**]*

Others deduce that due to a lack of world knowledge (no voting experience) they will have difficulty adapting to some of the roles available:

*[my role boundary issues are **not having the previous relevant knowledge** or understanding]*

The trainees ongoing questioning and exploration of their role and its boundaries, is to be expected, as Mindess reminds us that *"It is not surprising that a field as young as ours has not come to a consensus about exactly what our role entails. … As our profession matures, we will undoubtedly redefine and refine our role many times."* (1999:13)

4.3 Audience

During their programme of study the trainees will have become familiar with the notion of 'audience' and their potential linguistic and cultural requirements. Though the translation brief for this particular assignment, has concise information with regards to the intended audience (see appendix text brief), the trainees nevertheless make a range of assumptions in regard to the audience their translation will serve. This is in part due to the fact that they are not in face to face contact with Deaf clients and therefore have no option but to build up a mental picture of their mostly unknown receptor audience and their potential diversity. This practice has also been confirmed by Ruuskanen when examining what professional translators do, *"When first asked directly if they addressed their translations to an imagined reader or audience, most professional translators replied in the negative. When questioned more closely about their working practices, however, it became apparent that* they did in fact construct such an audience...They were often surprised to realise that they had evidently been doing this all of their working lives." (1996:233). Nevertheless, the physical absence of an audience, poses challenges for the 'co-construction of meaning' (Angelelli, 2001; 2003) translators/interpreters would aim to achieve.

The thoughts of the trainees reveal that they are aware that Deaf people will not have access to information in their first language, the very access we often take for granted. This will be particularly important for those Deaf people who are about to obtain the right to vote for the first time:

> [It is possible that some of the Deaf community may not know much about how to vote as their **native language is BSL and not English**]
> [The target audience would be **18+ or approaching 18** and be BSL users]

Their thoughts also indicate that they take into consideration that Deaf people's sign language use can be mapped on a continuum ranging from native language ability to acquired language ability, with linguistic influences from the host community's language, namely English:

> [The translation will need to cover a range from **visual modality to English** in order to be **accessible to all generations**]

> *[It can be **presumed** that the **audience's language** level is of a **good standard**...people from different ends of the **spectrum** (SSE/BSL)]*

They acknowledge that this can result in varying levels of sign language proficiency amongst Deaf people and can map contrasting syntactical features onto the sentence construction within their language use. The medium of distribution of their end product (the internet) makes them question the language variety in existence within the community:

> *[The audience...are likely to understand **basic BSL**]*
> *[I have chosen to use a **medium level of BSL**]*
> *[...my text could be accessed by anyone **nation wide**...wide range of BSL users]*

This language variety is compounded by the result of a range of sociolinguistic influences, which have a direct impact on the linguistic features produced by Deaf people at vocabulary and syntactical levels:

> *[**regional signs** may be needed]*
> *[DEAF PEOPLE LIVE LONDON...all **ages, genders and social class**]*

The thought processes of the trainees show that they contemplate the English language proficiency of their Deaf clients. This educational attainment has been well documented (Conrad, 1979; Powers, Gregory, &

Thoutenhoofd, 1999; Powers, 2007; CRIDE, 2012; NDCS, 2012, 2013) and is often referred to as the 'attainment gap':

*[we can assume they have a **good grasp of English**]*

Stone argues that *"The translation decisions ... hearing translators and interpreters make about the audience... should be examined in terms of what (and how) [language] is interpreted"* (2009:44). Our trainee interpreter's thoughts focus mainly on language proficiency of the intended audience, and hence evidence these very 'decisions' that will create the language in the end product.

4.4 Rhetorical questions

Rhetorical questions are questions to which the answer is not expected to be provided by the audience, the answer will be either provided by the speaker or signer or the answer is assumed to be common knowledge. The thought processes of the trainee interpreters show a proliferation of rhetorical questions in their thinking. What is also of interest, is that in contrast to thoughts about the previous thought categories discussed, which were expressed in their A language (English), thoughts involving rhetorical questions are expressed directly into their B language (BSL). This is evidenced within their write aloud protocols, by the use of sign language glossing conventions often utilised by sign linguists (see below).

According to our observations, made during many years of training interpreters, we noticed that trainees (in particular CODAs) tend to overuse rhetorical questions in their English to BSL interpretation, even though rhetorical questions, as a linguistic feature, undeniably occur more frequently in BSL than English.

> [ECONOMIC DEVELOPMENT MEAN WHAT?], [HELP HOW?], [VOTE WHEN?], [WANT VOTE?],
> [THINK NOT SURE BEEN REGISTER? REGISTRATION FINISH WHEN?], [RESPONSIBLE
> CONTROL MANAGE WHAT?] , [MAYOR RESPONSIBLE WHAT?], [14 BILLION BUY WHAT?],
> [LONDON ASSEMBLY RESPONSIBLE WHAT?], [WANT VOTE LONDON?] , [POLICING DO WHAT?], [USE FUNDING FOR WHAT?], [COMMONWEALTH WHO INCLUDED?] , [VOTE HOW? VOTE WHO?], [BUDGET WHAT FOR?], [MORE INFO WANT?...VOTE ALL?], [PROXY WHAT?]

The trainees in their linguistic and sign language modules have had ample opportunity to analyze the natural use of rhetorical questions in BSL discourse and apply it in their BSL production, but the moment they switch to any translation/interpreting mode, the natural function of rhetorical questions transmutes to take on a range of additional functions. Livingston, Singer & Abramson (1994) found that the use of rhetorical questions leads to a more successful interpretation as it enhances the opportunity for greater understanding by a Deaf audience.

Naturally occurring rhetorical questions can function as a means of introducing new lexical concepts, be used as transition markers and often signal the introduction of important information. In addition to these functions, the trainees utilise rhetorical questions to: reinforce concepts, educate the audience, inform about instructions/choices, list multiple options, segment the text, and pause in order to create additional processing time. This is supported by the result obtained by Livingston, Singer & Abramson in their study, who claim that interpreters use rhetorical questions *"to signal main and transitional points in the text"* (1994:189) and not only *"to emphasize key points … but also to show contrast and to exemplify"* (1994:191).

It can also be an indicator of the 'effort' required, as Gile pointed out *"Differences between the syntactic structures of the SL and the TL can increase the memory effort's processing capacity requirements because of the waiting involved before being able to reformulate the SL segment into the TL."* (2002:170) and goes on to explain that *"Languages with a limited vocabulary and a rather rigid grammar that imposes strict conditions on the order of elements in the sentence as well as grammatical agreement conditions could be associated with higher production effort requirements"* (2002:173). Rhetorical questions can therefore be an indicator that the translator is about to restructure the source language text to make accommodation for the target language and the target audience.

4.5 Glossary

Many of the thought processes are linked to vocabulary dilemmas, this may in part be due to the fact that the participants in this study are not yet qualified interpreters, but also links to Gile's (2002) point made above, that languages whose vocabulary range does not match, require greater 'processing effort':

> *[requires **extra** thinking on how to sign this successfully in BSL]*

We will take an extract from the chosen text 'Voting information': *"You can vote if you are aged 18 or over on 23rd May 2014, if you are a British, Irish, Commonwealth or European citizen and you live in London."* and focus on the concept 'Commonwealth'. Very quickly we find proof of a central premise in interpreting, namely, if you cannot understand the message in the source language, you cannot interpret it in the target language. It identifies the gap between the trainees' current world knowledge and Janzen's argument that *"The successful working interpreter requires a vast, almost encyclopaedic, knowledge..."* (2005:3):

> *[needs further research into how to sign correctly and efficiently]*
> *[need to do research in order to have a better understanding]*
> *[this term may cause some concern]*

Several trainees put the responsibility for the world knowledge back onto the target audience, though others suggest making adjustments given the specific needs of the audience:

> [Fingerspell, if you are in it you will know, if you are not, it will be inconsequential to them]
> [I am unaware which countries make up the commonwealth, but as the text does not list them, I think it may be superfluous for me to do so]
> [will need additional explanation to meet the audience's language requirements]

The thoughts of other trainees confirm that some see new concepts as a barrier, because they are expecting a direct equivalent to exist, and an established sign is unknown to them:

> [I am unsure about how to sign this]
> [generic sign?]
> [may be difficult to explain in translation]
> [it's a tricky word]
> [recognised vocabulary may not exist and therefore I will have to find a way to sign the concept]
> [it is not something I have seen discussed often by the Deaf community]

Their thought processes also reveal specific translation procedures that the trainee would follow in order to sign their end product. This relates specifically to where there are already established linguistic procedures to introduce a new concept into BSL (sign formation). This is often a phased process, for example, fingerspell + explanation + coined sign (productive lexicon), but may not include all phases:

> [*a voluntary association of 53 countries, this concept may need to be fingerspelled, and then a little information provided as to what it actually is to ensure clarity*]
> [*fingerspell C-O-M-M-O-N-W-E-A-L-T-H and explain what it is*]
> [*It is vital to explain what it is so that my audience can relate*]
> [*this concept may need to be explained*]
> [*don't go into too much detail, but specify it's a group consisting of other countries*]
> [*may require productive lexicon or explanation*]
> [*sign AREA and W reinforce with fingerspelling*]

The thought processes also indicates that, the trainees that have either, a greater world knowledge, or have carried out, a more extensive preparation, have an ability to go beyond a basic explanation:

> [*A country that was once part of the British Empire for example New Zealand and Australia*]
> [*a group of 54 countries (including the UK) work together to help each economy and follow the same human rights agreed between all of the countries*]

AIIC (2013) strongly advocate the sharing of glossaries as solutions can be found in the glossaries, or in our case, in the 'minds' of other translators. This is reflected in the thoughts of one trainee, who envisages more experienced practitioners as a resource base:

> *[consult with more experienced signers]*

The exercises we carry out during the interpreting programme and the thoughts documented by the trainee interpreters in this study clearly illustrate AIIC's view that *"Glossary preparation is an important learning process, the main point of which is to help you understand and memorize the terminology."* (AIIC 2013)

5. Conclusion

This study highlights that TAPs/WAPs are a suitable method for gaining access to the thought processes which lie/hide behind the many decisions made in the translation process. Within the cohort which took part in this research, certain thought categories proved to be predominant. These were thoughts in relation to: vocabulary, understanding and the target language audience, which may in part reflect the current stage of their training development, but similar categories are also found in more experienced translators (Bown & Dekesel 2011, 2012).

The prevalence of thoughts about their audience resulted in a preference for 'radical translation approaches' (Nord,

1991), which were often in direct contrast with the professional translators modelling the same text. When questioned on this issue, most trainees responded that literal translations should not be viewed as translations as they show little evidence of active thought processes and variation in translation strategies.

A more surprising response came from Deaf Interpreter educators and Deaf people, who upon viewing the anonymous data from the collective mind, quickly started using the thoughts evidenced, as playing a key part in whether they would book a particular interpreter for an assignment. This could support the argument that there is a tendency amongst some Deaf individuals to prefer an interpreter's attitude over their quality output.

Participants within the study generally indicated that the collective mind approach benefitted their development as interpreters. This indicates that there is merit in examining the process in favour of the end product. It helped reaffirm both the views of Séguinot (1997) and Bellos (2011) that they should move away from insisting on one solution to a particular translation problem, and instead explore the range of acceptable alternatives, provided in this instance by others within the collective mind.

Accessing the thoughts of other translators also confirmed for them that the text posed hurdles, which were commonly experienced by others in their cohort. The myriad of glossary solutions which they could peruse, allowed them to extend their own knowledge and asserts AIIC's (2013) recommendations. Their online access patterns and behaviour, best described by Salmon (2006), who compares the interaction of learners with a virtual learning environment, by comparing them to the behavior of animals, were persistently displaying 'magpie' characteristics (copying the thoughts of others and declaring them as their own).

The thought processes gathered provide an intriguing insight into the contrast between theoretical models of effort versus the actual distribution of effort between the different thought categories. It also documents that translators actively think in their target language (BSL) whilst undertaking a translation. The trainees involved reported that the 'collective mind approach' in which they took part, which coincided whilst they were studying other modules on the programme, enhanced their analytical ability to undertake those modules. Specifically in the areas of: restructuring, working through translation problems, text analysis and learning through collaborative working. These can be seen as transferrable skills.

As interpreter educators, during the course of the study, the collective mind approach enabled us to
gain access to the predominance, absence and quality of certain thought processes. This allowed us to intervene at an individual and cohort level, and pinpoint specific personal developmental needs of individual trainees. We were in a position to influence their thoughts, and provide alternative options, *before* they became actions. For example, by

augmenting their: language proficiency, comprehension of source language texts, awareness of the range of strategies available, role boundary considerations, continuing professional development requirements; which ultimately contributes to their future fitness to practice.

Our study was initially designed to look inside the mind of an interpreter 'in training', but one might equally argue that there is merit in considering it 'post –training' as a continuing professional development tool. We would therefore recommend that a *collective mind approach* should be included in all interpreter training programmes, as it can be part of *"...the purposeful creation of situations from which the motivated [and unmotivated] learners should not be able to escape without learning or developing."* (Cowan, 1998:112)

References

AIIC (2013) Practical Guide for professional conference Interpreters. http://aiic.net/page/628

Anderson L. (1994) Simultaneous interpreting: contextual and translation aspects. In Lambert, S. & Moser-Mercer, B. (eds) *Bridging the gap: empirical research in simultaneous interpretation.* Amsterdam: John Benjamins, pp. 101-120.

Angelelli, C. (2001) Deconstructing the invisible interpreter: a critical study of the interpersonal role of the interpreter in a cross cultural/linguistic communicative event. (Doctoral dissertation, Stanford University). *Dissertation Abstracts International, 62,9,2953*.

Angelelli, C. (2003) The visible collaborator: interpreter intervention in doctor/patient encounters. In *From topic boundaries to omission: new research on interpretation*, Metzger, M., Collins, S., Dively, V. And Shaw, R. (eds.) pp3-25 Washington DC: Gallaudet University Press.

Avval, S. (2012) Communication Strategies in Translation: A Review on the Taxonomies from 1977 to 2011. In *Journal of Siberian Federal University - Humanities and Social Sciences*, 5:6, pp. 768-779.

Bellos, D. (2011) *Is that a fish in your ear? The amazing adventure of translation.* London: Penguin books.

Bernardini, S. (2001) Think-aloud protocols in translation research: achievements, limits, future prospects. In *Target* 13:2, pp. 241-263.

Bown, S. & Dekesel, K. (2011) Phased by translation. Paper presented at EFLSI 2011 'Sight translation, sight interpreting meeting at the cross modes: sign language interpreters as translators, Vietri sul Mare, 16th-18th September, manuscript.

Bown, S. & Dekesel, K. (2012) Phased by translation: identifying the challenges and solutions in sight interpretation. in Cardinaletti, A. (Ed.) *Sight translation, sight interpreting meeting at the cross modes: sign language interpreters as translators* Marston Gate: Amazon, pp. 23-33.

Capper, J. (2001). *E-learning growth and promise for the developing world.* TechKnowLogia, Available at http://www.techknowlogia.org

CiLT (2006) *National Occupational Standards in Interpreting.* London: CiLT

CiLT (2010) *National Occupational Standards in Interpreting.* London: CiLT

Cokely, D. (1986) Effects of lag time on interpreter errors. *Sign Language Studies* 53, pp. 341-376

Cokely, D. (1992) The Effects of lag time on interpreter errors. in Cokely, D. (ed) *Sign Language interpreters and interpreting.* Burtonsville, MD: Linstok Press, pp. 39-69.

Conrad, R. (1979) *The Deaf School Child.* London: Harper & Row, 1979.

Cowan, J. (1998) *On becoming an innovative teacher: reflection in action.* Maidenhead, UK: Oxford University Press.

CRIDE (2012) Consortium for Research into Deaf Education report on 2012 survey on Educational provision for deaf children in England. http://www.ndcs.org.uk/professional_support/national_data/uk_education_.html

Ericsson, K. & Simon, H. (1984) *Protocol Analysis: verbal reports as data.* London: The MIT Press

Gile D. (2002) Conference interpreting as a cognitive management problem in Pöchhacker F. And Shlesinger M. (eds.) *The Interpreting Studies Reader.* London: Routledge, pp. 162-176.

Jääskeläinen, R. (2002) Thin-aloud protocol studies into translation: an annotated bibliography. In *Target* 14:1, pp.107-136.

Janzen, T. (Ed.) (2005) Introduction to the theory and practice of signed language interpreting. In Topics in

Signed language interpreting: theory and practice. Amsterdam: John Benjamins, pp. 3-24.

JISC (2008) *Exploring tangible benefits of e-Learning: does investment yield interest?* Newcastle upon Tyne: Northumbria University.

Keegan, D. (2000) *Distance training: taking stock at a time of change.* London: Routledge Falmer.

Krings, H. P. (1986) *Was in den Köpfen von Übersetzern vorgeht.* Tübingen: Narr.

Krings, H. P. (1987) The use of introspective data in translation. In Færch, C. And Kasper, G. (eds.) *Introspection in Second Language Research.* Clevedon: Multilingual Matters, pp. 158-176.

Li, D. (2004) Trustworthiness of think-aloud protocols in the study of translation processes. In *International Journal of Applied Linguistics* 14:3, pp.301-313.

Livingston, S., Singer, B. and Abramson, T. (1994) A study to determine the effectiveness of two different kinds of interpreting. In Winston, E. (Eds) (1995) *Mapping Our Course: A Collaborative Venture. CIT Convention 1994-Proceedings.* Charlotte, North Carolina: CIT, pp. 174-203.

Llewellyn-Jones, P. & Lee, R. (2014) *Redefining the role of the community interpreter: the concept of role-space.* Marston Gate: Amazon.

Mindess, A. (1999) *Reading between the signs: intercultural communication for sign language interpreters.* Yarmouth: Intercultural Press.

NDCS (2012) *NDCS note on Department for Education figures on attainment for deaf children in 2011 (England),* London: NDCS

NDCS (2013) *Stolen Futures: an investigation into the spending cuts facing deaf children 2010-2013* http://www.ndcs.org.uk/search_clicks.rm?id=6882&destinationtype=2&instanceid=350763

Nord, C. (1991) *Text analysis in translation: Theory, methodology, and didactic application of a model for translation-oriented text analysis.* Amsterdam: Rodopi.

NRCPD (2010) *Code of conduct for communication professionals.* http://www.nrcpd.org.uk//page.php?content=30

Powers, S. (2007) *The Educational Attainments of Deaf Pupils: A discussion Paper on Data Currently Available.* http://www.batod.org.uk/index.php?id=/resources/research/nat-data.htm

Powers, S., Gregory, S. and Thoutenhoofd, E. (1999) The educational achievements of deaf children: a literature review – executive summary., in *Deafness & Education International*, 1:1, pp 1-9.

Radović-Marković, M. (2010) Advantages and disadvantages of E-learning in comparison to traditional forms of learning. In *Annals of the University of Petroşani, Economics,* 10(2), pp. 289-298.

Roffe, I. (2002) E-learning: engagement, enhancement and execution. In *Quality Assurance in Education* 10:1, pp.40-50.

Russell, D. and Winston, B. (2014) Tapping into the interpreting process: using participant reports to inform the interpreting process in educational settings. In *Translation & Interpreting* 6:1 pp.102-127.

Ruuskanen, D. (1996) Creating the 'Other': a pragmatic translation tool. In Dollerup, C. & Appel, V. (eds) *Teaching translation and interpreting 3: new horizons*. Amsterdam: Benjamins, pp. 233-241.

Salmon, G. (2006) *E-tivities: the key to active online learning*. London: Routledge Falmer.

Sampaio G.R.L. (2007) Mastering sight translation skills, in *Tradução & Comunicação*, No 16, pp.63-69.

Séguinot, C. (1997) Accounting for variability in translation. In Danks, J. Et al (eds) *Cognitive processes in translation and interpretation*. London: Sage publications, pp.104-119.

Shirvani, K. (2009) On the Applicability of Oxford's Taxonomy of Learner Strategies to Translation Tasks. In *The Journal of Applied Linguistics,* 2:1, pp. 216-237.

Smith, A. (2014) Think aloud protocols: viable for teaching, learning, and professional development in interpreting. In *Translation & Interpreting* 6:1, pp. 128-143.

Stone, C. (2007) Deaf translators/interpreters rendering processes: the translation of oral languages, in *The Sign Language Translator and Interpreter* (SLTI), Volume 1:1, pp. 53-72.

Stone, C. (2009) *Toward a Deaf translation norm*. Washington D.C.: Gallaudet University Press

Thurmond, V. A., Wambach, K., & Connors, H. R. (2002). Evaluation of student satisfaction: determining the impact of a web-based environment by controlling for student characteristics. *The American Journal of Distance Education*, 16(3), pp. 169–189.

Tiene, D. (2000). Online discussions: a survey of advantages and disadvantages compared to face-to-face discussions. *Journal of Educational Multimedia and Hypermedia*, 9(4), pp. 371–384.

Tirkkonen-Condit, S. and Jääskeläinen, R. (eds) (2000) *Tapping and mapping the processes of translation and interpreting.* Amsterdam: John Benjamins.

Van Doorslaer, Luc (2007) 'Risking conceptual maps', in Yves Gambier and Luc van Doorslaer (eds) The Metalanguage of Translation , special issue of *Target* 19:2, pp. 217–33.

Vygotsky, L. (1978) *Mind in Society: The development of higher psychological processes.* Cambridge, MA: Harvard University Press.

Zhang, D., Zhao, J. L., Zhou, L., & Nunamaker, J. F., Jr. (2004). Can e-learning replace classroom learning? *Communications of the ACM*, 47(5), pp.75–79.

Appendix

Translation Brief: You have been commissioned by the offices of the Mayor of London to produce a British Sign Language translation of 'Voter information for BSL users' for people living around London who use BSL and can vote for the Mayor of London. The signed text will be transmitted via the web during the election campaign.

Voter information for British Sign Language users

On 23rd May 2014, people living around London can vote for the Mayor of London and the 25 members of the London Assembly. The Mayor and Assembly are responsible for many aspects of everyday life in London, including transport, policing, the environment, housing and economic development. The Mayor makes decisions with the aim of improving the city and lives of Londoners. The Mayor is also responsible for an annual budget of over £14 billion pounds which goes towards transport around London, policing and the fire brigade.
The London Assembly is made up of 25 people, it looks closely at the work of the Mayor to see that they meet their promises and deliver good value for Londoners. The Assembly puts questions to the Mayor and investigates important issues for Londoners.

You can vote if you are aged 18 or over on 23rd May 2014, if you are a British, Irish, Commonwealth or European citizen and you live in London. You need to be registered to vote by

18th April, if you are not registered or you are not sure if you are registered, visit the website or contact your local council. You can vote in one of three ways; firstly you can vote at your local polling station – polling stations are open between 7am and 10pm on 23rd May 2014. Secondly, you can apply for a postal vote. The deadline for applying for a postal vote is 18th April 2014. Lastly, if you are unable to get to a polling station, you may appoint a proxy. This means asking someone you trust to vote on your behalf. The deadline for applying for a proxy vote is 25th April 2014.

Nearer the election, every registered voter in London will receive an information booklet. This will list all the candidates and help you understand how to vote. If you would like more information, visit our website, or send us your enquiry by email or text.

please note this text has been adapted for the purposes of this research.

Sign Language Interpreting, challenges, tactics and efforts

Sophie Pointurier-Pournin, Ph.D.,
ESIT, Université Sorbonne Nouvelle – Paris 3
sophie.pournin@hotmail.fr

This conference is devoted to the cognition from the perspective of the performer. So I naturally wanted to share some parts of my research, particularly the analysis of the cognitive load when the interpreter is translating from spoken to sign language. I conducted my research in Translation Studies under the direction of Professor Daniel Gile, who has developed several models of interpretation (consecutive, simultaneous, translation, sight translation) in the early 80's, to explain the difficulties regularly faced by students or professionals. The model I chose to work with is the Effort Model of simultaneous interpretation which was first designed for spoken languages and spoken interpreters. One of the goals of my research was to study its transposition to sign language interpreting, to see whether and how it could be transposed, and to observe the differences and the similarities in the interpreting tactics from a cognitive perspective.

In order to understand this model we will first present:
- Automatic activities and Attentional Resources
- The Effort Model of simultaneous interpreting in spoken languages

- The specific challenges in SL interpreting, with an overview of the main constraints and tactics
- The transposition we made of the Gile's Effort Model regarding sign language interpreting

1. **Automatic activities and Attentional Resources**

To understand the Effort Model we have to know what is an Attentional Resource. To understand what is exactly an Attentional Resource we have to know the difference between an automatic operation and a non-automatic operation.

Gile's work is based on cognitive literature and researches automatic versus controlled operations. Daniel Kahneman made a very interesting contribution on this subject that you can easily find in his book *"Thinking fast and slow"*. The main theory explains that in everyday life, your brain is dealing with all the information you can encounter in two different ways: with your *System 1* or with your *System 2*.

The System 1 = Automatic operations:
***"System 1** operates automatically and quickly, with little or no effort, and no sense of voluntary control."* (D. Kahneman, 2011:24)
Automatic operations are natural, instinctive, fast, and they don't require any conscious operation or effort (i.e.: detecting that one object is more distant than another, detecting hostility in a voice/face). But some conscious

operations like foreign language proficiency may become automatic through repetition (i.e.: foreign language proficiency: *dog* in English is *chien* in French, or basic mathematics: 2 + 2 =4). All this means, that the brain reacts automatically and gives a response without any cognitive pressure.

The system 2 = Non automatic operations
*"**System 2** allocates attention to the effortful mental activities that demand it, including complex computations. The operations of system 2 are often associated with the subjective experience of agency, choice, and concentration."*
(D. Kahneman, 2011:24)
The operations here are demanding concentration and efforts. In that way, these operations are slower and require a minimum of processing capacities and Attentional Resources. We can see that speech production for example, or comprehension or discourse analysis, is handled by System 2.

Interpreting is NOT an automatic operation, as speech production cannot be automatic; comprehension is not automatic and the discourse analysis is not automatic because there is no possible automation through repetition: it's never the same discourse we have to translate. Only some parts of discourse can become automatic, like introductions. For example: *Ladies and gentlemen we are very happy to welcome you...* are chunks that your brain recognises through regular exposure and can therefore handle instantaneously.

We have to keep in mind that Efforts and Attentional Resources are necessary for interpreting but unfortunately for us, Attentional Resources are limited.

2. The Effort Model of simultaneous interpretation in spoken languages (Gile, 1995)

- **Reception Effort (R):** Listening and Analysis Efforts
- **Memory Effort (M):** Short Term Memory (information storage before deciding or not to integrate them in the target discourse)
- **Production Effort (P):** Production of speech in the target language (including self monitoring)

These three efforts are in competition because of limited Attentional Resources

- **Coordination Effort (C):** Distribution of processing capacities between each Effort. This effort may be particularly important according to recent researches.

Simultaneous interpreting = R + M + P + C

According to Gile, this model is not strictly scientific nor idealistic or prescriptive. **It is not designed to describe the interpreting process.** It's an explanatory framework focusing on cognitive **constraints and limitations** (excluding 'social' or 'ideological' constraints and limitations, etc.). This model must be taken as a tool for teaching the interpreting process.

The Reception, Memory and Production Efforts are not automatic as it's never the same content interpreters have to deal with, and they never have the same amount of information to deal with. Coordination Effort is not automatic either, as management of Attentional Resources is always different, in that way it cannot be repeated.

The usual misunderstanding about this model is that sometimes, trainers ask their students to "train" their "efforts management". Because interpreting is not an automatic operation this is by nature impossible and absolutely not the purpose of the model (see Gile 2009 or Pointurier Pournin 2014). You cannot decide to give a certain amount of your processing capacities to one effort in particular, it is always changing. The only thing you can achieve with practice is to reduce the need of Attentional Resources given to one task by being familiar with a specific discourse (scientific for example).

Because of limited Attentional Resources, the total processing capacities requirement for interpreting should not exceed the interpreter's total available processing capacities. That simply means that you can't give more than you have.

In general, interpreters are working close to saturation and cognitive overload (the 'tightrope hypothesis', Gile: 95). The idea is to understand that when interpreters work close to saturation, it's not a problem of personal insufficiencies, but it's because they are facing chronic cognitive tensions between processing capacities supply and demand during their performance (too fast, too technical, etc.). However, training can enable them to reduce attentional requirement for a task.

3. Personal research: observing the constraints and the tactics

I wanted to observe SL interpreting as it occurs in reality, and not as the main professional assumptions usually explain how it has to be. My data has been obtained from 3 different empirical studies involving 18 French sign language interpreters (students, experienced interpreters and very experienced interpreters), in order to analyse the kind of phenomena which could be arising and whether they were due to a lack of practice or to a technical challenge in the interpreting process. My first surprise was to realise that experienced practitioners and students had to face the same challenges. The phenomena were not the consequence of a lack of practice, but could be considered as a part of the constraints and challenges of sign language interpreting in general. Following closer observation and with combined data (corpus of 18 situations of interpretation analysis and 18 interpreters' interviews visioning their own production; focus groups with a larger sample of interpreters; integration of two other empirical studies), I analysed the cognitive challenges of translational tactics that SL interpreters naturally favoured.

Assuming that interpretation is closely linked to constraints, I analysed when problems occurred, which were the interpreter's tactics for getting through them, and how much attentional resources those tactics were demanding of the interpreters.

Between signers in dialogic situations, time is not a constraint for signing and when constructing paraphrases. But when you are in the situation of interpreting time pressure is one of the biggest issue. Of course this must be analysed regarding the constraint of time as it is the main constraint in interpreting.

3.1. *The constraints*

What are the main constraints in sign language interpreting? The first ones are maybe the norms and rules that were never empirically analysed. I suppose this is the main obstacle for a better understanding of our profession which has a lot of rules and norms: they can be linguistic, norms about behaviour in a professional setting, social conduct, or the financial organisation of our profession, etc. But are those rules applicable all the time?

The main challenge is that sign language interpreting is a new profession which wanted to be normalized very quickly in a political sensitive context (recognition of sign language as an official language like the national language of the country, claiming for SL in deaf education, etc.). In that sense, we were not necessarily afforded the luxury of time to undertake the empirical research to explore the SL interpreting process as it occurs in the reality. We directly deemed as a political and very understandable act – that sign language interpreting was identical to the translational process in any other linguistic combination syntactically far apart.

The profession is young, and still wants to be recognized and seen like conference interpreting in spoken languages. A lot of professional norms (as ethics or linguistic norms) were established in a very short period of time, and my intuition was that maybe we had much more norms than regarding conference settings. So I analysed how all those norms may have an impact on the SL interpreter's production.

First, I found that all these challenges (affective, social, linguistic, etc.) are very common topics in the literature of translation studies in spoken languages. But when it comes to sign language interpreting, those constraints are not recognized as such and they usually must be handled through the interpreter's personal skills. But, as they are considered as professional constraints in spoken languages, I just analysed them as such in the SL interpreting process. Constraints lead the interpreter to chose one or several tactics, and this choice has an impact on the interpretation process (cognitive, production).

Example of constraints during the interpretation:
Linguistic constraints: lexical gap between French and LSF (one million words in French including technical vocabulary, 5000 or 6000 signs in SL)
Social-professional constraints:
- Lexical gap is a sensitive subject "it does not exist in SL" (although it does in any other languages).
- A hearing SL interpreter cannot create signs.
Situational constraint: time pressure in simultaneous interpreting

Example of tactics observed:
  - A visual paraphrase in SL.

What is the impact on the production?
In the heat of the moment, the interpreter has to find a quick (visual) definition and this action requires mental energy.

In my research, I found that more than more than 50 percent of the consecutive segment following a lexical gap had major deteriorations (omission, wrong meaning, etc.).

3.2. *Tactics observed in SL interpreting*

There may be tactics that you already know or experienced as discursive tactics in SL, but I chose to name them, drawing on translation studies literature and not on linguistic concepts. These tactics must be understood as a response to a translational challenge.

I will focus today on the tactics that are different from the ones generally observed in spoken languages.

- **Scene Staging** (scenarization) *"Scene staging is anything but a realistic description of an actual experience. It consists of imagining a scene which condense the sense."* (Séro-Guillaume, 2008). This is a tactic adapted for SL interpreting from Seleskovitch and Lederer Theory of the sense.

This research highlighted that there are two kind of scene staging: one which is **directly derived from the speech** and a **creative** one when lexical gaps occurs for example.

Scene staging derived from the speech: the SL interpreter is using space with all the elements or entities that are clearly in the speech. The interpreter creates interaction in the signing space.

My empirical observations show that in general it does not occur spontaneously, as the interpreter needs a trigger (pronoun, explanation, repetition of the idea in the speech) to construct their signing space.

Creative staging: is the production of a translation that gives a definition, an explanation of the words that have no lexical correspondence in the target language (SL).

My empirical observations show there are several steps for its production:

1. Conceptualisation : understanding the concept
2. Defining staging units: identifying relevant elements from the conceptualization that could generate interaction.
3. Space modelization (spatial mapping)
4. Actual staging: imagination, creation of the interaction.

This has nothing to do with the idea of "creating a mental picture" of the discourse. Mental pictures are just a part of the comprehension process. Scientists showed that mental pictures are strictly personal, they move, they are mixed with your own feelings and experiences (Arnheim, 1976). It's not a mental screen that can be transposed into your own signing space (Kosslyn, 1980).

▶ **Fingerspelling:** is not accepted as a relevant linguistic element in LSF (French linguistic constraint and norm)

Fingespelling demands a huge amount of cognitive resources: the empirical observations show a lot of omissions on the following chunks (spillover effect, see Gile) which means that the problem arises not in the segment that was difficult, but is transposed to subsequent segments. The interpreter gave all his mental energy to the task (production) and had to 'recharge' to continue to listen or store in short memory, he needs a few seconds to keep up.

I noticed that all the tactics that the French SL interpreters naturally favoured were cognitively extremely demanding and, regarding the interpreting laws, their behaviours are different from those of the general interpreting community.

4. **Adaptation of the Effort Model to Sign language interpreting (from a spoken discourse to sign language production)**

Regarding all the real constraints that the SL interpreter must deal with, the Gile's Model can be adapted to the modalities of sign language interpreting. This is not a merely linguistic approach, considering the fact that translation studies focus on the interpreter's global constraints (linguistic, social, emotional, etc.) under the pressure of TIME.

Below I present the adaptation of the model to French Sign Language interpreting, which could probably be extended to sign language interpreting no matter the national spoken or sign language used.

Reception Effort (R): no major differences with spoken languages interpreting.
Memory Effort (M): we add the Memory of Space (see below).
Production Effort (P): we add Creative Staging Effort (see above), contextual indications and spatial mapping memory.
Space management Effort (S): a new effort specific to SL interpreting. It integrates working, contextual spaces, and

direct interactions with the interpreter during their production (with the speaker/signer/assembly).
Coordination Effort (C): no major differences with spoken languages interpreting.

From a translation studies perspective, as D. Seleskovitch has often highlighted, the situation of communication is a decisive factor for the interpreter's translational decisions.

In my research, I found that when the interpreter is using contextual indications (pointing out someone who is speaking, noise, humour, etc.), they add information that enable the deaf person to be part of the interpreted event (confirmation of the sociolinguistic works of C. Wadensjö (1998), M. Metzger (1999), C. Roy (2000), and J. Napier (2002)). The nature of these choices has an impact on the production effort. **Space management Effort** is an Effort on its own in SL interpreting.

In SL interpreting, relevant information is not only present in the interpreter's signing space. It may be useful to consider the linguistic space as a part of the global contextual space: as sign language is by nature a visual language, real space interferes but also sometimes is integrated to sign language production. Signers often use the deictic pointing to point out an element in their signing space in order to specify the subject or reactivate a part of speech. They can also point out an element present in the room to integrate the information in the flow of the speech. Even if it can be seen as a regular linguistic phenomenon in dialogic talk between signers, this notion is very interesting as the contextual space of enunciation becomes an important part of the interpretation production to be managed by the interpreter. Regarding the interpreter's signing space, the "Spatial Mapping Memory" increases the "Memory of Space".

Compared to simultaneous interpretation between spoken languages, interpretation in SL allows a greater availability at the beginning (the two modalities are not in conflict, we can hear the speech and sign). This cognitive availability is very quickly reassigned to other highly intensive cognitive tasks such as the ones I listed in this presentation.

References

ARNHEIM, R. (1976) *La pensée visuelle*, Paris : Flammarion.
GILE, D. (1995) *Regards sur la recherche en interprétation de conférence*, Presses Universitaires de Lille.
GILE, D.(2009) *Basic Concepts and Models for Interpreter and Translator Training*, (Revised Edition), Amsterdam/Philadelphia: John Benjamins Publishing Company.
KAHNEMAN, D.(2011) *Thinking Fast and Slow*, New York: Farrar, Strauss and Giroux.
KOSSLYN S.M.(1980) *Image and mind*, Cambridge, MA, Harvard University Press.
METZGER, M.(1999) *Sign language Interpreting: Deconstructing the myth of neutrality*, Washington, D.C: Gallaudet University Press.

NAPIER, J.(2002) *Sign Language Interpreting, Linguistic coping strategies*, Coleford England: Douglas Mc Lean.

POINTURIER-POURNIN, S. and GILE, D. (2012) Les tactiques de l'interprète face au vide lexical, *Jostrans*, vol 17, pp164-183.

POINTURIER-POURNIN, S.(2014) *L'interprétation en langue des signes française: contraintes, tactiques, efforts*, Thèse de doctorat de traductologie, ESIT, Université Sorbonne Nouvelle – Paris 3.

ROY, C. (2000) *Interpreting as a discourse Process*, Oxford/New York: Oxford University Press.

SELESKOVITCH, D. et LEDERER, M.(2002) *Pédagogie raisonnée de l'interprétation*, deuxième édition revue et augmentée. Paris : Didier Erudition.

SERO-GUILLAUME, P.(2008/2011) *Langue des signes, surdité et accès au langage*, Paris, Editions du Papyrus.

WADENSJÖ, C. (1998) *Interpreting as interaction*, London: Longman.

"Oil on troubled waters": a metaphorical perspective on interpreting and politeness

Rachel Mapson
University of Bristol
mail@rachelmapson.com

Introduction

This paper about metaphors, politeness and interpreting forms part of my doctoral study into how British Sign Language (BSL)/English interpreters identify and interpret polite language from BSL to English. Here, my discussion focuses on some of the metaphors used around politeness and interpreting. These relate both to the language transfer and 'dialogue management' (Sandrelli 2001) aspects of interpretation. The data reported, illustrate how metaphor can be a useful tool to facilitate description of politeness in signed language and the way politeness relates to interpreting.

Politeness is not an easy subject to research because our knowledge about it is generally tacit. In our first language (L1) we generally acquire politeness implicitly (see Blum-Kulka 1997), and it is seldom taught explicitly in second language (L2) learning environments; this is reflected in the experiences of BSL/English interpreters for whom BSL is L2 (Mapson forthcoming). However, this is potentially problematic for interpreters because our knowledge about politeness is likely to remain tacit, or implicit, unless we make a conscious decision to examine it in detail. My research indicates the benefits of a more explicit focus on politeness in relation to our work.

Linguistic politeness

There are many definitions of linguistic politeness, but Sachiko Ide's definition of "language associated with smooth communication" (Ide 1989: 22) resonates closely with our work as interpreters and the way we facilitate communication between our clients.

Perhaps the best known literature on politeness is the politeness theory developed by Brown and Levinson (1987) in which politeness is considered as an inherent property of specific linguistic forms which are used to show respect to others. Their work has been followed by discursive models of politeness, for example the work of Locher and Watts (2005) and the rapport management theory of Spencer-Oatey (2005, 2008). These discursive approaches emphasise the dynamic nature of politeness, how relationships are played out through language and how politeness is created in interaction rather than being a property of particular words and phrases.

Politeness in signed language

The abundance of literature on linguistic politeness in spoken language is not reflected in the work on signed language to date. The earliest work to focus on politeness in signed language is that of Lucinda Ferreira Brito's study on LIBRAS (1995), though unfortunately her work may have been overlooked because it is not published in English. George (2011) conducted a doctoral study on politeness in Nihon Shuwa, but the majority of research has been conducted in the USA. Between them (Roush 1999, 2007) and Hoza (2001, 2007, 2008) identified five key non-manual markers relating to linguistic politeness in ASL.

I conducted some preliminary research into linguistic politeness in BSL (Mapson 2013, 2014) to underpin my research on interpreting politeness. The results suggest that non-manual features are also the key means of conveying politeness in BSL; the six most-used politeness features in BSL, involving use of the upper face, mouth and head/upper body are summarised in Table 1. Some of these features are shared with both ASL and Nihon Shuwa. These politeness markers relate to some of the metaphors created by the interpreter participants in my research.

Table 1: Six key non-manual features for politeness in BSL

Articulator	*Non-manual feature*
Upper face	Raised brows
	Semi-closed eyes
Mouth	Tight lips
	Polite Grimace
Head and upper body	Side tilt
	Polite duck

Interpreting politeness

There is relatively little literature on interpreting politeness. Much of the literature relating to spoken language interpreting concentrates specifically on analysis of legal interpreting, predominantly focussing on court settings (Berk-Seligson 1990, Hatim and Mason 1997, Mason and Stewart 2001, Hale 2001, Angermeyer 2005, Nakane 2008).

In contrast, the literature on signed language interpreting is more diverse, with Hoza (2001) examining employment related situations and Savvalidou (2011) analysing the signed interpretation of political speeches in Greece. Additionally, although not focussed specifically on politeness, issues concerning politeness are included within Banna's (2007) analysis of interpreting at a committee meeting, Major's (2012) work on healthcare interactions and Dickinson's (2014) study of workplace interpreting.

Metaphor, politeness and interpreting

This paper explores how politeness and interpreting can be described through metaphor. Metaphors are expressions that conceptualise or describe one thing in terms associated with something else. They are commonly used to help describe abstract concepts in ways that are easier to understand. Many scientific concepts are expressed through metaphor for this reason. However, metaphors don't only help our understanding but can also influence and limit the way we think about things (Lakoff and Johnson 1980, Arundale 2013).

In their influential work on metaphor, Lakoff and Johnson (1980) describe different types of conceptual metaphor. These include orientational metaphors (for example the general notion that good is up and bad is down), ontological metaphors (such as the idea of the mind being a machine – 'my mind isn't working well today') and structural metaphors where one activity is described in words associated with another (for example, 'oh, I see' meaning 'I understand')[1]

Krippendorff (2009) lists six conceptual metaphors that are used in relation to communication. One of these is the idea of communication as a hydraulic system, and relates to expressions such as 'the flow of communication'. There are connections between this metaphor and those expressed by the participants in my research.

Metaphor has also been discussed in relation to politeness in both spoken and signed languages, with one metaphor bridging the modality divide. Both Werkhofer (1992) and Watts (2003) discuss the notion of politeness as capital, or money, something that is exchanged in interaction. Similarly Roush (2011) talks about conceptual metaphor in relation to politeness in ASL and the idea that polite

---

[1] These examples are English-based and may not transfer effectively into other spoken languages

interaction is conveyed through signs that involve mutual exchange.

Within interpreting studies there is literature that explores the various ways metaphor can be translated from one language into another (Newmark 1982, Schäffner 2004, Roush 2015), but metaphors also appear within discussion about the process of interpreting and how interpreters work. One metaphor that conceptualises the process of interpreting is the outdated notion of the interpreter as a conduit (Reddy 1979, Roy 1992), while Angelelli (2004) explores a number of metaphors that relate to the different functions interpreters adopt.

If, as literature indicates, metaphors can influence our thinking, then our use of metaphors can help evidence our thinking. The metaphors that interpreters use when talking about interpreting politeness may therefore reveal useful insights about how politeness relates to our work.

Data

Data were generated through a series of semi-structured group discussions involving two groups of BSL/English interpreters, all with a minimum of ten years of interpreting experience. One group comprised four CODA[2] interpreters for whom BSL is their L1, the other group learned BSL as L2. I met each group on three occasions over a five-month

---

[2] Children of Deaf Adults (CODA)

period and later met participants again to feedback initial findings from the data. Those feedback discussions generated further data.

The metaphors that participants used were not prompted by specific questions and emerged naturally during the discussions. Participants used metaphor for two main purposes:

- as metalanguage, to create labels for linguistic features for which they lacked specialist vocabulary
- to describe conceptual aspects of politeness in relation to their work

The following discussion focuses on these two distinctions.

Metaphors as metalanguage

Prior to my research, there was no published literature on linguistic politeness in BSL. This meant that the interpreter participants in my study lacked a specialist vocabulary to use in their discussions of the subject. They overcame this difficulty in two ways. Firstly, they demonstrated politeness in BSL, and then they used metaphoric labels for the demonstrated features in their ongoing discussions. The metaphors generated by the participants can all be related back to the key non-manual features identified for politeness in BSL (Mapson 2013, 2014).

Wallace and Gromit was used as a label for the *polite grimace*; one participant described it as "that Wallace and Gromit look". This metaphor is a reference to two animated characters that star in a number of films made by Aardman Animations Ltd. This visual reference is so striking that both groups of participants independently generated the same metaphor for this feature.

The *side tilt* was described with the metaphor of *The Titanic*[3], creating an image of the ship tilting to one side as it sank. This metaphor was instigated by Henry[4], one of the CODA participants, but subsequently adopted by others, as was the case with many of the metalinguistic metaphors. For example, when watching video footage of a Deaf signer, Maurice asked "does he do a little bit of Titanic there?"

Churchill was a metaphor created to refer to the *polite duck*. This metaphor relates to an animated bulldog with a nodding head that features on television adverts for car insurance in the UK.

The combination of a *polite duck and side tilt* was referred to as *Richard III*, a former King of England renowned for his spinal deformity.

These metalanguage metaphors, all of which draw on strong visual images from popular British culture, formed effective

---

[3] The Titanic was a trans-Atlantic liner that sank in 1912 with tragic loss of life.
[4] Participants selected their own pseudonyms to be used in publication of the research.

descriptors of the non-manual features used for politeness in BSL and facilitated participants' discussions about politeness in BSL and how it might be interpreted.

Metaphors to conceptualise politeness in interpreting

Participants illustrated their understanding of politeness through the use of conceptual metaphor; they used metaphor when defining politeness and when discussing the interpretation of politeness. Metaphors were also used when considering politeness more generally in relation to our work and professional conduct. Three dominant metaphors that emerged were *politeness as a lubricant*, *politeness as packaging*, and *interpreting as plastering*. A common theme throughout these three conceptual metaphors is that politeness facilitates smooth communication.

Politeness as a lubricant
Participants used the conceptual metaphor of *politeness as a lubricant* in relation to politeness generally. For example, Maurice uses this metaphor when explaining the purpose of politeness.

> *The more fundamental point is, why is politeness important for anybody? And I assume it's about people in crowded situations, or in touch with other people, it's the oil that enables us to live together peaceably. (Maurice)*

This idea of politeness as a lubricant fits well with Krippendorff's hydraulic metaphor of communication; it also mirrors Ide's (1989) definition of politeness as something that enables smooth communication.

The concept of politeness to lubricate and facilitate communication can be developed further to consider the cultural mediation (Alexieva 1997) necessary when interpreting between Deaf and hearing clients. Participants described how they soften spoken interpretations to what they consider appropriate in the target language.

> *Well, it's the thing that we put down as cultural mediation, but it maybe isn't that, but we feel the need to, soften it, sometimes, for the hearing audience. (Jean)*

Data indicate that frequently what participants described as cultural mediation has to do with adjustments concerning what is polite in the target language, and how this use of politeness facilitates smooth communication between Deaf and hearing clients.

The idea of politeness as a lubricant was also related to our behaviour as professionals, and a tool that can be used to our advantage.

> *I think for an interpreter, politeness is important because that social oil makes your job easier. (Maurice)*

Politeness as packaging

The notion of *politeness as packaging* was a second conceptual metaphor generated by participants. Olly's comment considers politeness to relate to the way a message is packaged, ensuring that it is appropriate both for the contents and the context. His comment concerns a Deaf person asking a question at the end of a plenary presentation. The question could have been perceived as a challenge to the presenter but was not, because of the way it was framed.

> *The Deaf person dressed it up really well [...] it was packaged in a way that is no way offensive. (Olly)*

If a message is packaged well, using appropriate language, it is more likely to be received positively. The idea of politeness as packaging was also related to interpreting. Participants acknowledged that sometimes when we interpret, we package things in such a way that the end product looks better than the original. Emma's example concerns an interpreted telephone conversation.

> *The reason for making the telephone call was because he was wanting to get a positive result. He had something that he wanted this person to do, and he was throwing in things like the Equalities Act because it was seemingly not getting where he wanted it to get, so he was then throwing those things in at the end. But I*

> think it would have been packaged better. So I took [laughs] yes, I stepped in and did some packaging. (Emma)

The idea of politeness for packaging a message, to make it more palatable to the recipient, is similar to the metaphor of *politeness as a lubricant* in which politeness is used to ensure smooth communication. It illustrates the importance of relational work (Locher and Watts 2005) and how interpreters' choices impact on this process.

Interpreting as plastering
A third conceptual metaphor in relation to interpreting politely is *the interpreting as plastering* metaphor generated by Angus. Angus uses this metaphor both in relation to the dialogue management responsibilities of turn-taking and to interpreting from English to BSL more generally.

> I had to put in lots of politeness, and I had to get my plastering trowel out to smooth over the turn-taking [...] and I think I do a similar thing when I'm voicing over [...] to perhaps smooth over cracks or make the cultural exchange seem more palatable to both sides. (Angus)

This metaphor of interpreting as plastering resonates with the smoothing and covering images created in the metaphors of *politeness as a lubricant* and *politeness as packaging*.

Conclusion

The use of metaphor by the participants in this study exemplifies their resourcefulness in language use. They had an immediate need to describe features of politeness in BSL, but their lack of specialised terminology led them to create effective metaphors to facilitate their discussion. However, data reveal the potential value of explicit knowledge about politeness and the terminology to enable articulation of that knowledge, suggesting a greater focus on this within interpreter training programmes could be beneficial.

The conceptual metaphors that emerged from participants' discussion on interpreting and politeness help evidence their understanding and perceptions of what politeness is and how it relates to their work. These metaphors illustrate how, though rarely discussed explicitly, politeness is integral within all aspects of interpreting. How we interpret politeness is important, but so too is how we interpret politely and how we conduct ourselves as professionals.

Acknowledgements

I would like to thank Dr Rachel Sutton-Spence and Dr Helen Woodfield for their ongoing support, Frankie McLean and Gary Quinn for producing BSL material for use during the interviews and to Dr Christopher Stone for his comments on an earlier version of this paper. Thanks also to all the Deaf people involved in my BSL study and to the interpreter participants for their enthusiastic engagement with my research.

References

Alexieva, Bistra (1997) 'A Typology of Interpreter-Mediated Events', *The Translator: Studies in Intercultural Communication* 3 (2): 153-174

Angelelli, Claudia (2004) *Medical Interpreting and Cross-Cultural Communication*, Cambridge: Cambridge University Press

Angermeyer, Philipp (2005) 'Who is 'you'? Polite forms of address and ambiguous participant roles in court interpreting', *Target* 17 (2): 203 226

Arundale, Robert (2013) 'Conceptualizing 'interaction' in interpersonal pragmatics: Implications for understanding and research', *Journal of Pragmatics* 58: 12-26

Banna, Karin (2007) *Interpreting and Gender: A Case Study*, Sydney: Macquarie University dissertation

Berk-Seligson, Susan (1990) *The Bilingual Courtroom: Court Interpreters in the Judicial Process*, Chicago: University of Chicago Press

Blum-Kulka, Shoshana (1997) *Dinner talk: Cultural patterns of sociability and socialization in family discourse*, Mahwah, NJ: Lawrence Erlbaum

Brown, Penelope and Stephen Levinson (1987) *Politeness: Some Universals in Language Usage*, Cambridge: Cambridge University Press

Dickinson, Jules (2014) *Sign language interpreting in the workplace,* Coleford: Douglas McLean Publishing

Ferreira Brito, Lucinda (1995) *Por uma Gramática de Línguas de Sinais* [For a grammar of sign languages]. Tempo Brasileiro

George, Johnny (2011) *Politeness in Japanese Sign Language (JSL): Polite JSL expression as evidence for intermodal language contact influence*, University of California, Berkeley doctoral dissertation

Hale, Sandra (2001) 'How are Courtroom Questions Interpreted?' in Ian Mason (ed) *Triadic Exchanges: studies in dialogue interpreting*, Manchester: St Jerome Publishing, 21-50

Hatim, Basil and Ian Mason (1997) 'Politeness in Screen Translating', in Basil Hatim and Ian Mason (eds) *The Translator as Communicator*, London: Routledge, 65-80

Hoza, Jack (2001) *The Mitigation of Face Threatening Acts in Interpreted Interaction: Requests and Rejections in American Sign Language and English*, Boston University doctoral dissertation

Hoza, Jack (2007) *It's Not What Sign, it's How You Sign it: Politeness in American Sign Language,* Washington DC: Gallaudet University Press

Hoza, Jack (2008) 'Five Nonmanual Modifiers That Mitigate Requests and Rejections in American Sign Language', *Sign Language Studies* 8 (3): 264-288

Ide, Sachiko (1989) 'Formal forms and discernment: two neglected aspects of universals of linguistic politeness', *Multilingua* 8 (2/3): 223-248

Krippendorff, Klaus (2009) *On Communicating Otherness, Meaning and Information,* London: Routledge

Lakoff, George and Mark Johnson (1980) 'The Metaphorical Structure of the Human Conceptual System', *Cognitive Science* 4: 195-208

Locher, Miriam and Richard Watts (2005) 'Politeness theory and relational work', *Journal of Politeness Research* 1(1): 9-34

Major, George (2012) *Not just 'how the doctor talks': Healthcare interpreting as relational practice,* Macquarie University doctoral dissertation

Mapson, Rachel (2013) Politeness in British Sign Language: the effects of language contact, in Alasdair Archibald (ed) *Multilingual theory and practice in applied linguistics: proceedings of the 45th annual meeting of the British Association for Applied Linguistics (BAAL)*, London: Scitsiugnil Press, 167-170

Mapson, Rachel (2014) 'Polite appearances: how non-manual features convey politeness in British Sign Language', *Journal of Politeness Research* 10(2): 157-184

Mapson, Rachel (forthcoming) 'Paths to politeness: Exploring how professional interpreters develop an understanding of politeness norms in British Sign Language and English' in Barbara Pizziconi and Miriam Locher (eds) *Teaching and Learning (Im)politeness*, Berlin: de Gruyter Mouton

Mason, Ian and Miranda Stewart (2001) 'Interactional Pragmatics, Face and the Dialogue Interpreter', in Ian

Mason (ed) *Triadic Exchanges: Studies in Dialogue Interpreting*, Manchester: St Jerome Publishing, 51--70

Nakane, Ikuko (2008) Politeness and Gender in Interpreted Police interviews, *Monash University Linguistics Papers* 6 (1): 29-40

Newmark, Peter (1982) *Approaches to Translation*, Oxford: Pergamon Press

Reddy, Michael (1979) 'The Conduit Metaphor: a case of frame conflict in our language about language', in Andrew Ortony (ed) *Metaphor and Thought*, Cambridge: Cambridge University Press, 284-324

Roush, Daniel (1999) *Indirectness Strategies in American Sign Language: Requests and Refusals*, Gallaudet University MA dissertation

Roush, Daniel (2007) 'Indirectness Strategies in American Sign Language Requests and Refusals: Deconstructing the Deaf-as-Direct Stereotype', in Melanie Metzger and Earl

Fleetwood (eds) *Translation, Sociolinguistic, and Consumer Issues in Interpreting*, Washington DC: Gallaudet University Press, 103-156

Roush, Daniel (2011) 'Language Between Bodies: A Cognitive Approach to Understanding Linguistic Politeness in American Sign Language', *Sign Language Studies* 11 (3): 329-374

Roush, Daniel (2015) *The translation of Event-Structure Metaphors rendered by Deaf Translators from English to American Sign Language*, Gallaudet University doctoral thesis

Roy, Cynthia (1992) 'A Sociolinguistic Analysis of the Interpreter's Role in Simultaneous Talk in a Face-to-Face Interpreted Dialogue', *Sign Language Studies* 74: 21-61

Roy, Cynthia (2000) *Interpreting as Discourse Process*, Oxford: Oxford University Press

Sandrelli, Annalisa (2001) 'Teaching Liaison Interpreting', in Ian Mason (ed) *Triadic Exchanges: studies in dialogue interpreting*, Manchester: St Jerome Publishing

Savvalidou, Flora (2011) 'Interpreting Im/politeness Strategies in a Media Political Setting' in Lorraine Leeson, Svenja Wurm and Miriam Vermeerbergen (eds) *Signed Language Interpreting: Preparation, Practice and Performance,* Manchester: St Jerome Publishing, 87-109

Schäffner, Christina (2004) 'Metaphor and translation: some implications of a cognitive approach', *Journal of Pragmatics* 36 (7): 1253-1267

Spencer-Oatey, Helen (2005) 'Rapport management theory and culture', *Interactional Pragmatics* 2 (3): 335-346

Spencer-Oatey, Helen (ed) (2008) *Culturally Speaking: Culture, Communication and Politeness Theory*, London: Continuum

Wadensjö, Cecilia (1998) *Interpreting as Interaction*, London: Addison Wesley Longman

Watts, Richard (2003) *Politeness*, Cambridge: Cambridge University Press

Werkhofer, Konrad (1992) 'Traditional and modern views: the social constitution and the power of politeness', in Richard Watts, Sachiko Ide and Konrad Ehlich (eds)

Politeness in Language: Studies in its History, Theory and Practice, Berlin: Mouton de Gruyter 155-199

Interpreting concerts

Rafaela Cota Silva
rafasilvalgp@gmail.com

Introduction

This work is based on a live performance experience which was the sign language interpretation of concerts by a Portuguese band called The Gift. Those shows took place in four different cities in Portugal, namely Lisbon, Oporto, Leiria and Coimbra and it happened during 2012.

In this paper we start by explaining the Portuguese deaf community's situation at the moment, and talk about their fights and, also, their achievements. Next, I will describe the relation between music, the feelings that it gives to us and how music exists in a deaf person's life. After that, we'll explain how it worked in the live performance: we start with the preparation of the interpretation before the concert, then the show and finally we'll consider the importance of feedback in order to improve the work. In this part, we'll greatly focus on the interpretation process, the techniques that we use to work with three different languages at the same time and the influence the environment has during the performance. Lastly, we'll reflect on the importance of this kind of event for the deaf community, especially the empowerment that they achieve through it.

This was a relevant experience because on one hand it was the first time that it happened in Portugal and, on the other hand, it was a situation which brought cultural access to the deaf community, as well as equality of opportunity and also a chance to show how sign language can be an art form. Besides that, this can serve as a model for other interpreters that may eventually do the same work in the future.

Theoretical basis

Currently, it is evident that modern society is very concerned with inclusion for all. This can be been for example in museums with increased access for people with visual loss, also the more visible architectural adaptations for those with reduced mobility. The barriers for the deaf community are not physical, therefore, sometimes it can be hard to make some changes that will include this minority. In order to provide full access to this information, the deaf community requires linguistic adaptation which includes sign language.

The deaf community all over the world and also in Portugal lived for years behind the oppression of not being able to express themselves in their natural language, the Portuguese Sign Language (Carvalho, 2007). In order to end that situation, the deaf community, sign language interpreters, deaf students', parents and teachers, came together to campaign which resulted in the recognition of Portuguese Sign Language (PSL) in the Republic Constitution, in 1997, namely "proteger e valorizar a língua gestual portuguesa, enquanto expressão cultural e instrumento de acesso à educação e da igualdade de oportunidades"[5] (Portuguese Republic Constitution, article 74º, point 2, paragraph h).

A deaf person's life is always marked with the existence of all kinds of barriers such as access to communication, information, education, public services and cultural events. On the other hand, with sign language, deaf people can be fully functional citizens with a culture and identity which defines them. Besides that, people of the same community who use Portuguese Sign Language (PSL) have a strong feeling of belonging to that group. Friedner & Helmreich (2012, p. 80) wrote that "such articulations of language, culture, and sociality foster new forms of affiliation as well as new senses of self and belonging".

Therefore, it is a society's responsibility to understand that all the settings in which deaf people are involved, should be accessible to them if the information is translated into sign language. It may seem a little strange that a context which involves music can be appealing for deaf people, however, "the common assumption that deaf culture is a culture without music has been a misjudgment made by many people in the hearing population" (Darrom & Loomis, 1999, p89). The same authors add that this brings "(...) a new dimension to the existing data on the topic of music and

---

[5] Protect and valorize portuguese sign language while cultural expression and education access tool and equality of opportunities. *N.T.*

deaf culture" (Darrom & Loomis, 1999, p.107) and the reason is "(...) because it represented a deaf people in a 'positive way' rather than as 'poor, pathetic people who can't hear music" (Darrom & Loomis, 1999, p.107). Summers (2012, p.1) also contradicts common sense saying that "music has been a part of many deaf people's lives. Music is and has been a part of Deaf Culture, including (...) sign language interpreters' function within live vocal music performances".

Sign language music interpretation has grown a lot. Examples of this can be seen on Youtube where with a simple search it is easy to find music videos with sign language from different countries (Maler, 2013).

This kind of performance where sign language is associated with music, either in videos or live, is innovative because it features and shows the importance of a cultural and linguistic minority. Also, with this, there is the benefit of changing the prejudice that the majority have when they think that music is only for those who can hear. Ament (2010, sp) says that "there is a notion that music is only heard and thus, can only be appreciated by the hearing. However, deaf people have a unique and challenging perspective to music that has seldom been explored outside of deaf communities". Besides, when we allow deaf people to access music in their natural language, sign language, we are at the same time, according to Maler (2013, p. 9) adding value to "(...) how deaf people hear, feel, and see music".

Besides the advantage of having equality of opportunity, concerts with sign language interpretation "(...) is an art form that combines important products of two cultures that have traditionally remained quite separate (...). Their intersection in song signing provides us with an invaluable opportunity to build stronger connections between hearing and Deaf (...)" (Maler, 2013, p.9). So, another point of view of events of this type is allowing the hearing and majority community to be more alert and sensitive to the deaf community, and that is possible because these events are for "(...) those with no knowledge of sign language to fluent and native" (Maler, 2013, p.9). Furthermore, it promotes a communication between the two communities because it brings them to the same space which encourages their interaction (Friedner & Helmreich, 2012). Thus, on one hand equality is been developed and, on the other hand, there is a movement against discrimination.

The process of interpretation

As I already mentioned this performance happened in four different cities in Portugal. It was very interesting to observe and verify that, from city to city, the audience changed, which also influences the way the interpreters approach their work. For example, in Lisbon, where deaf people are more used to having performances with sign language interpreters, they were more receptive and there were a lot of deaf people in the audience interacting with the interpreter and using the signs to sing. In Coimbra, a University city, there were a huge number of young deaf people who actually like to go out at night to places which have music. Those people are used to feeling music and they were really enjoying the concert. These kinds of aspects like audience feedback can be very relevant when analyzing the interpreter's work (Colonomos, 1992).

In regards to this, the interpretation of concerts involves many aspects during the performance that don't exist in other interpretation contexts, for instance, the show's environment, music rhythm, cadency, tone of voice, instrumental characteristics, the double meanings of audience, audience feedback, etc. About that, Maler (2013, p. 2) says that "song-signing performances comprise four principal forms of expression: music, lyrics, the signs of ASL[6], and other gestures independent of the signed language (i.e. dancing, swaying, pulsing, etc.)". Summers (2012, p. 39) adds that "though the lyrics themselves are an important aspect of a signed performance, incorporating elements from the sound created by the music are important to effectively interpret the piece".

Besides the interpretation itself, this kind of performance has to have some particularities which are fundamental for deaf people to get a good perception, namely, of the place where the interpreter is located, the lighting, visibility and also the working conditions where the interpreter is placed (McIntire & Sanderson, 1995).

---

[6] American Sign Language.

In this particular situation, the interpreter was managing three different languages: English, Portuguese and Portuguese Sign Language. So, how does the mind feel when working with these three languages? What steps does the interpreter go through to get into the target language and how do they occur in his/her mind?

In order to do this work, the interpreter needs to do a good preparation of the interpretation. At the time of the proposal of having concerts with the addition of sign language, the band The Gift were releasing a new CD called "Explode" which included a book with a photo report made in India. Those pictures were taken during the Holi Festival, which celebrates the arrival of spring and where people throw each other colorful balloons and that's the reason why this festival is also known as the festival of colors. The band decided to incorporate that spirit and had a lot of stage decorations with colors. The band clothes were also very colorful so, in order to fit the show and to be in tune with the message and in the consultation with the event organizers the interpreters decided to choose colorful clothes.

So, the first thing to do was to look at the images of the CD and understand the purpose and the reason why every song had a specific image. Do the images have a special connection to the songs/music or were they just selected randomly? It was very important for the interpreters to know that, so that they could really grasp the meaning of the lyrics.

As stated, this band sings in English so all the lyrics were written in that language which isn't the first language of the interpreters. The next step was translating the lyrics into Portuguese. Once this preparatory work was completed by two interpreters, we took some time to discuss the lyrics and the perception that we each had. At this point, while we were analyzing the lyrics we had to deal with metaphors, hidden meanings or some specific vocabulary that we were not aware of. So, doubts were unavoidable and because we wanted to make sure that we understood it correctly, we had a meeting with the band in order to clarify all the questions that were not clear to us. Also that meeting was crucial to understand the logic and the goals of some lyrics or sentences, the general ideas, the double meanings and to get an opinion of how the band wanted some information to be passed on to the audience.

After that discussion, we made an interpreting proposal and we tested each other by one of the interpreters doing the sign language while the other one observed without hearing the music. The purpose here was to test the translation with a partner and see if it made sense. We discussed the signs that corresponded directly to some words or expressions and we looked at alternatives that would be more suitable. That preparation is fundamental to the interpreters' performances and that is because our minds think in a different way so it's important to share our interpretation choices and work as a team. At this point, we can't forget that we are a part of the discourse since we made choices, subjective choices that are influenced by ourselves. In other words, we have many options and we choose the ones that make more sense to us and that we think will be well perceived by the audience. We were dealing, all the time, with subjective choices that we needed to make and inter-subjective things to deal with, like how our mood, our feelings and our thoughts related to the music or about the environment at the performance moment. Additionally we needed to be very careful with the choices we made because that would reflect in the discourse that we produced and, obviously, in the information that deaf people in the audience would have access to, because deaf people were "reading" that situation through the interpreters. As Friedner & Helmreich (2012, p. 73) said "Deaf people are first, last, and all the time the people of the eye".

Interpretation by itself is already a complex task (Brunson, 2004) and in this kind of context it's even harder because, as mentioned before, there were three languages being used at the same time: English as the language that was sung, Portuguese, the cognitive working language converting English into Portuguese sign language, and Portuguese Sign Language, which was the language produced by the interpreter. Taking these processes into account, the question to be asked is; How does the mind deal with this level of complexity and simultaneous interpret?

In order to be able to do this, the interpreters should have a good knowledge of English, the source language, otherwise they couldn't translate something that they don't understand. It's necessary to understand the source message and then, because that language isn't our mother language, our mind automatically, does the translation to Portuguese. At this point the interpreters were working with what is called 'mental language' and that is because the language that is used to translate and decode the source language is not the language that will be produced in the target form. The mental language is kept in the mind and that is done in order to understand the message (Colonomos, 1992). In this situation, the interpreters had already prepared the source text which means that the mental language was ready for the task. In this situation what happens is a process of consecutive interpretation and the reason is that although the interpretation is happening simultaneously, it has been prepared. In this kind of interpretation, the interpreters had already heard what they had to translate, and had had enough time to understand the message and prepare it, so it wasn't being undertaken live, simultaneously and unprepared.

As previously mentioned, Portuguese was the language that interpreters use only mentally but which wasn't produced in the target language. Portuguese plays a very important role in this situation because it was the language that connects the other two languages. It was the language that the interpreters employ to analyze and encode the message. Besides that, it was also the language that they use to test if they understand the message because if the mind was able to translate the source, it means that what was heard was understood. Beyond that, the mental language here was substantial in order to organize the information in the mind, to select lexical items to be produced, to know how it is going to be explained and also to manage the process between the other two languages. That process of management always happens during linguistic interpretation, but in this specific situation, the management was done by a language which stays only inside our mind.

At the same time that the mind translates the source language to the mental language, it is already starting to be translated into the target language. So, it's there, in the mind, that we begin to perceive if what is produced, will be an accurate equivalent target message.

Finally, we used the mental language to find the linguistic equivalents between the source language and the target language, which means that the process to go from one language to the other one occurs, all of it, in the mind (Cokely, 1992). When the interpreters had completed the mental exercise they are ready to convert it into the target language and, in this case, what was produced was, clearly, influenced by the preparation that they had done before.

It's very interesting to analyze and realize that what actually happened during the interpretation was that new ideas, at the time, were becoming apparent. In addition to the preparation made before, the mind was continuing to find new interpretation choices and while the interpreters were producing sign language they noticed that they had an alternative way to transmit the idea which, at that moment, seemed better. That is very common while interpreting because the professionals are not machines, and frequently their actions are influenced by the audience's feedback or just by facial expressions which informs them whether the message is making sense (Stewart, Schein & Cartwright, 1998). But, what happens in the 'black box' that makes the interpreters change at that moment, the target or the discourse that they had prepared before? That is a very important aspect to reflect upon when it happens, because our mind is so full of tricks that set off alarms or gives us a clue that if we chose another way the target language produced could potentially be better? The human mind is powerful and it has many abilities to manipulate languages.

When performing, interpreters are active members once they make linguistic choices which will affect the ones who receive the language. Nevertheless, interpreters always intend to produce the target message as clearly and as faithfully as possible with the aim of constructing meaning as clearly and faithfully as possible for the receptor audience i.e. deaf people. Interpreters hear the vocabulary, the grammar, process to understand and extract the meaning and then make linguistic decisions about vocabulary, grammar and sentence structure in the target language.

In this situation, when the interpreters have heard the information contained in the song, they carry out a live simultaneous interpretation, which means that the process occurs at that precise moment.

So, during the process of interpreting and dealing with languages, what problems or potholes can our mind suffer from? Also, what can influence the mind and the performance itself? Certainly, one fundamental aspect is the knowledge of the subject. In this particular case knowing the lyrics was very important to the interpreters so that they were able to organize their ideas and have the correct tools prepared to ensure a good performance. Not understanding what was said is one aspect which can be very complicated for the interpreters because if they don't understand it, they can't translate it. So what should they do in this situation especially because they can't interrupt to ask for clarification? Should they leave the audience with an information gap? In this particular case the situation was not easy because there was a lot of background noise, such as people clapping and screaming and decoding the message became a cognitive challenge. Fortunately, the interpreters weren't working alone but in a team so the partner who wasn't translating at the moment would notice that and lend a hand by feeding signs to the actively working interpreter.

Another aspect are the rapid choices the interpreter has to make and the realization that one choice wasn't the best option and then changing it if there is the time and ability to process the concept in question. It depends upon the complexity of the incoming message and the processing time being used. That happens because interpreters are, without noticing, always evaluating themselves. Also their feelings can influence the interpretation because the interpreter's mood can have an effect on their performance.

Besides that, the feelings of the people who are receiving the information are very important too. In this case, if the deaf people dance, if they clap, smile, jump or if they are sign singing together with the interpreter they are, at the same time, showing that they are enjoying and understanding. If the interpreter notices that the deaf audience isn't enjoying the signed performance, their mind will probably search for a new interpretation strategy which can attract more attention from the deaf audience. The audience responses send visual clues to the interpreter which in turn engergises the interpreter's performance and, unconsciously, their minds keep on doing the good work. Here the mental alertness is very significant because it is a part of the work. The mind needs to be focused on so many processes that are happening at the same time, for example, the vocabulary and the audience. However, on the other hand, interpreters can't allow their minds to lose concentration otherwise that will potentially cause the interpreter to omit information.

There are also some psychological aspects which should be taken into account whilst interpreting. For example, things related to the band like the rhythm, the cadency and the tone of voice. According to Maler (2013, p.4) interpreter's "(...) movements seem deliberate and dance-like is sufficient for understanding that there is a degree of conformance between music and the signer's gestures". Summers (2012, p.40) says that "(...) incorporating elements from the sound created by the music are important to effectively interpret the piece". Certainly music exists to stir up emotions in people and that's a personal experience to everybody. The interpreter must be very careful to avoid creating barriers on the way those emotions go through from the singer to the audience. This is an important issue and interpreters need to fit in with the singer so they can have as little influence as possible. To do that, the interpreters must match the linguistic environment and produce the language appropriately. Also, the speech needs to be not only linguistic but also nonverbal and that's done through body movement and expression. In addition to the musical features from the band there are others for example related to the interpreter's space; which should be near to the band or within the field of vision of both, and the lighting and visibility which have to be arranged and adapted for a deaf audience (note that the audience is likely to be mixed in their receptive requirements).

It is vitally important that interpreters evaluate their performance, not only during an interpretation but also post event. This process makes us think about our work, about our choices and about our performance. The musical context is no exception. So, after the concert the interpreters carried out an evaluation by asking themselves some questions like: What went wrong? What didn't work? What can we change for the next concert? What was good that we should maintain? What can we do to make the interpretation clearer? This individual and pair reflexive practice is fundamental to realize how successful the interpretations were. To realize what were the failures, to improve the performance and to be continually improving as part of their continuous professional development. It should be added that they had the chance to do that because their performance was recorded.

Conclusion

Although it's not very common to see shows with sign language in many places, it's a reality that has slowly been growing. The concern of the majority is in including all of the people that have different characteristics whether they are physical, cognitive or linguistic. There is still though, a long way to go. Nevertheless, if we a want fully inclusive society with active citizen participation, we need to give them the environment and opportunities which allow them to do so. Most of the time, it's not the minority that can't do anything, it's us who don't gave them the chance to do it.
Cultural access to all is a fundamental tool to building a more informed society and this can be achieved by ending social inequality. This also means including the deaf sign language using community. That is their primordial instrument which guarantees them inclusion.

Moreover, sign language can also be seen as an art form and these public performances are also important because of that. Maler (2013, p.3) reinforces that idea by saying that "(...) the signed song are an artistic outlet for anyone, deaf or hearing". If on one hand this brings the deaf community the feeling of empowerment and the opportunity to see and enjoy a concert in their own natural language; on the other hand, these performances are a way of showing sign language to hearing people. Some of these people may not have thought about the existence of sign language. The inclusion of sign language has the dual effect of raising awareness of the linguistic and cultural needs of the deaf community and makes sense in the musical domain because it isn't the "(…) hearing that makes the music. No, it's your heart. It's your body. It's your rhythm inside you that makes the music not your ears" (Summers, 2012, p.35).

Events which are fully inclusive to both deaf and hearing people make it possible to start the discussion about equality of opportunity. So we no longer have that well known "illusion of inclusion" (Russell, 2010) but a real situation of inclusion.

References

Ament, A. (2010). *Beyond Vibrations: The deaf experience in music*. Gapers Block. Chicago: Illinois. Available in http://gapersblock.com/transmission/2010/07/22/beyond_vibrations_the_deaf_musical_experience/ Accessed on the 6 of July 2015.

Brunson, J. Sign Language Interpreting: Moving Towards Professionalization. Embodied Workers Conference. New York: Syracuse. Available in http://faculty.maxwell.syr.edu/mdevault/JeremyBrunson.pdf Accessed on the 6 of July 2015.

Carvalho, P. (2007). *Breve História dos Surdos no Mundo*. Lisboa: SurdUniverso.

Cokely, D. (1992). *Interpretation: Towards a Sociolinguistic Model*. Burtonsville, MD.: Linstok Press.

Colonomos, B. (1992). *Processes in Interpreting and Transliterating: Making Them Work for You*. Westminster, CO: Front Range Community College.

Darrom, A. & Loomis, D. (1999). *Music and Deaf Culture: Images from the Media and Their Interpretation by Deaf and Hearing Students*. Journal of music Therapy, XXXVI (2). Pp. 88-109. Available in http://www.ncbi.nlm.nih.gov/pubmed/10519846. Accessed on the 20 of June 2015.

Friedner, M. & Helmreich, S. (2012). *Sound Studies Meets Deaf Studies. Senses & Society*. Volume 7. Pp 72-86. Available in http://web.mit.edu/anthropology/pdf/articles/helmreich/helmreich&friedner_sound_studies_deaf_studies.pdf. Accessed on the 21 of June 2015.

Maler, A. (2013). *Songs for Hands: Analyzing Interactions of Sign Language and Music*. MTO: A Journal of the Society for Music Theory, 19 (1). Available in http://mtosmt.org/issues/mto.13.19.1/mto.13.19.1.maler.pdf. Accessed on the 21 of June 2015.

McIntire, L. & Sanderson, G. (1995). *Who's in charge?: Perceptions of empowerment and role in the interpreting setting*. Journal of Interpretation, Pp 99-113.

Portuguese Republic Constitution. Chapter III. Cultural rights and duties article 74º Education, point 2, paragraph h.

Russell, D. (2010). *Illusion of inclusion? Realities and consequences*. Alberta, Edmonton. University of Alberta. Available in http://www.wccds.ualberta.ca/en/~/media/wccds/Documents/Resources/russell-nm-21.pdf Accessed on the 6 of July 2015.

Stewart, A.; Schein, D. & Cartwright, E. (1998). *Sign language interpreting: Exploring its art and science.* Boston: Allyn and Bacon.

Summers, A. (2012). *Deaf Culture and Music: The Role of Sign Language Interpreters within Live Music Performances.* Senior Theses. Paper 4. Available in http://digitalcommons.linfield.edu/muscstud_theses/4/. Accessed on the 21 of June 2015.

Abstracts of the conference

Consecutive and Simultaneous Interpreting: Research, Reality and Reflection

Keynote speaker: Debra Russell

This presentation will provide a context for the conference presentations that follow, by reviewing the research findings about consecutive and simultaneous interpreting in legal settings, and contrasting that with other studies from spoken language researchers. In a study of courtroom interpreting with experienced interpreters, the results demonstrated that consecutive interpreting was more effective than simultaneous interpreting when dealing with Deaf witness testimony and that a blend of consecutive and simultaneous interpreting was most effective when dealing with cross-examination of a Deaf witness and expert witness testimony (Russell, 2000, 2005). The results challenge the long-held belief that because there is no auditory interference for signed language interpreters, there is no need to work consecutively, and that simultaneous is the most accurate and preferred form of interpretation.

The results also invite interpreters to consider the training required to know how to make effective discourse based decisions that will meet the needs of the participants in a given interaction. Additional research explored the ways in which our teaching of "mind tricks" influences the ways in which consecutive and simultaneous interpreting is used in our field (Russell, 2002). Are we building on current research to ensure we are getting the skills we need for effective interpreting practice? For example, some programs approach the teaching of consecutive interpreting as a stepping-stone to simultaneous interpreting, never to be used once in the field. Other programs integrate consecutive interpreting as a form of interpretation to be used throughout one's career as an interpreter.

Building on research findings we will examine strategies for employing greater use of consecutive interpreting in our interpreter education programs, mentoring practices, and in our daily reality of making informed practice profession decisions in order to offer meaning-based interpretation.

"Cooking without recipes" - The cognitive processes and strategies applied by trainee sign language interpreters

Sarah Bown and Kristiaan Dekesel

There is an understandable obsession towards the end product created by interpreters, especially given that a tangible error analysis can be conducted to indicate the flaws. From an educational and developmental perspective, however, we are more interested in the choices that lead to this product, as its overall quality can be enhanced by 'manipulating' the thoughts behind the choices made (Bown & Dekesel, 2012), in order to achieve the ultimate goal which Nord defines as "what should be going on in a translator's mind" (1991:234).

Interpreter educators have long been fascinated by the interpreter's mind, but their thought processes are not easily demonstrated, as these can only be retrieved by embarking on a process oriented approach. In their attempts to access the 'black box' (make the invisible visible) researchers utilised Ericsson & Simon's think aloud protocols (Krings, 1986; Tirkkonen-Condit & Jääskeläinen, 2000) and, even embarked upon electroencephalogram (EEG) monitoring (Kurz, 1992), in their realisation that access to this box "could afford exciting insights" (Anderson, 1994:118).

This paper explores the documenting of thought processes, via the use of on-line forums (WOLF, 1996), which in turn enables educators to create a taxonomy of the strategies employed. Participants accessed the cognitive processes of their peers and provided feedback. This supports the idea of a social learning community (Vygotsky, 1978) and the co-construction of knowledge (Network Learning Manifesto, 2002).

Access to this collective mind was monitored through a tracking system, which facilitated the categorization of visible thoughts and also provided insight into an individual's potential training needs. Interviews with participants established the motivation behind accessing the minds of others, and the perceived benefits that access granted. The end aim was to equip interpreters with a diagnostic tool to visualise their own thoughts and help them evaluate possible developmental needs.

Stance Taking and Double Contextualization in the Interpreting Process

Terry Janzen and Barbara Shaffer

Language users continually employ perspective-taking in their discourse, choosing from various subjective lexical, grammatical and discourse options available to them. These choices are not without semantic and pragmatic consequences. They reflect the subjective and intersubjective stance of speakers and signers (Janzen and Shaffer 2008, 2013). Perspective-taking is expressed in a variety of alternations, e.g., active/passive constructions, direct/indirect speech, selection of moods such as the subjunctive, conditionals, etc., deixis and indexing, and contextualization. Motivations for perspective-taking choices are pragmatic, whereas their consequences are at the lexical, grammatical, and discourse level.

While in everyday discourse, speakers make perspective choices at a fairly unconscious level, interpreters are left to rely on discourse evidence to tell them what the speaker has attempted to accomplish, thus they must assess what constructions are being used and search comparable constructions in the target language that have similar effects.

Contextualizing in discourse takes place for pragmatic reasons. It is an intersubjective discourse activity where the speaker/signer chooses contextualizing information based on what she believes her interlocutor does not have access to but needs to know with the goal of making her discourse as clear as possible. Importantly, the interpreter must deal with contextualizing twice: once in the source speaker's text she apprehends, and once again in her own target text.

In this paper, we address both the function of double contextualization in the interpreting process and its effects. At times the interpreter's contextualizing well reflects that of the source speaker, and times when it does not, based on differences in linguistic structure or language ecology, the interpreter's assessment of intersubjective relationships in the interpreting triad or, in fact, the interpreter's own knowledge base. We draw from examples of interpreters' work when contextualizing source speakers' discourse, and offer insights into the interpreting process that can inform interpreting pedagogy.

Cognitive changes in interpreters as a result of sign language interpreter training and experience

Christopher Stone and David Vinson

This presentation will report on a longitudinal aptitude study following the learning trajectory of undergraduate students within Deaf studies and interpreting programs identifying the factors that are relevant for sign language learning and relevant for sign language interpreting. It will also compare these results with experienced interpreters (10+ years and full professional status) identifying those cognitive developments that occur during training and those that develop with experience.

A battery of tasks was administered to the undergraduates, which can broadly be split into five areas:

General language skills – Modern Language Aptitude Task (MLAT) administered semester one (five sub-tests)

General intelligence – digit span and matrix reasoning administered semesters one and six

L1 language skills – English reading age administered semesters one and six

L2 language skills – BSL grammatically judgement task (BSLGJT) administered semesters one, three, five, six

Cognitive tasks – connections A (psychomotor) and B (psychomotor and cognitive control), patterns (perceptual processing) and a flanker task (conflict processing) administered semesters three, five, six

This test battery was also administered to undergraduates in Deaf studies programs that included an interpreting specialisation (n = 22), a control group of undergraduates with no exposure to BSL and studying psychology (n = 21) and expert interpreters with 10 or more years' experience and full professional status (n = 14).

Initial analysis shows that learning BSL does enhance psychomotor skills, task switching and conflict resolution.

SL interpretation: challenges, tactics and efforts

Sophie Pointurier-Pournin

What happens in the head of the interpreter the heat of the moment? What are the challenges? What are the tactics of the interpreter and what are their impacts on the process of interpretation? Our demonstration is based on Daniel Gile's Efforts Model of simultaneous interpreting (1985, 1995 and 2009). This model relies on the notion of attentional resources and processing capacities developed in cognitive psychology. Simultaneous interpretation is not an automatic operation, as the realization of the process is controlled and requires "energy", which means attentional resources and processing capacities. All of the cognitive operations involved in interpretation can be grouped into subsets called "Efforts". They are three Efforts in this model: the Listening and Analysis Effort, the Production Effort, the Memory Effort, plus a Coordination Effort which corresponds to the resources required to coordinate the three other Efforts. Information processing is more or less flexible within each subset and depends on several factors: the interpreter itself, the technical nature of the speech, the flow of the speaker, etc. The "Tightrope Hypothesis" explains the model and states that problems occur when total processing capacity requirements exceed available processing capacity and when processing capacity available for a given effort is not sufficient for the task the interpreter is engaged in. The empirical approach of our research has allowed us to highlight several findings: first we identified the major SL interpreters' challenges (linguistic, social, space, etc.) and their impacts on the interpreter's production. Then, we focused on the main tactics available: paraphrasing, scenarising, borrowing, fingerspelling and transcoding. We analyzed the cognitive impact of these tactics on the general process of SL interpretation. Our conclusions allowed us to make a proposition of an adaptation of Gile Efforts' model applied to SL interpreting. The lecture will include the presentation of this model.

Use of signing space in simultaneous sign language interpretation: marking discourse structure with the body

Anna-Lena Nilsson

A fundamental difference between signed and spoken languages is that in signed languages the signer uses the three dimensional space in front of him/her (signing space) and his/her own body for reference and cohesion. Optimal use of signing space is dependent on the signer's knowledge of what s/he is going to talk about. In a simultaneous interpreting situation, there is no way the interpreter can know exactly what the speaker will say next. This makes it difficult for an interpreter working simultaneously into a signed language to know how to best structure the discourse.

In the present study, Swedish Sign Language (SSL) interpreters have been filmed while interpreting spoken Swedish monologues into SSL. Their signed language production was analyzed using a model based in Conceptual Blending Theory, focusing on their use of Real Space Blending (Liddell, 2003), and on how they use signing space and their body to mark the discourse structure.

In this presentation, I will show how interpreters whose first language is SSL consistently use specific body movement patterns to mark discourse structure. Despite finding out the discourse content only gradually, and while they are already rendering their interpretation of what has been said so far, these interpreters produce signed discourse that is strikingly similar to spontaneously produced SSL discourse. We will also see that these movement patterns are used even when there are no obvious lexical cues in the source text indicating that e.g. a comparison will be made.

In addition to providing new knowledge regarding use of signing space in signed language interpretation, this presentation also attracts attention to the challenge of how to best train L2 users of signed languages to become skilled interpreters.

Not Quite Utopia: Insights on Interpreting from Deaf Leaders on Three Continents

Karen Bontempo, Tobias Haug, Lorraine Leeson, Jemina Napier, Brenda Nicodemus, Beppie Van Den Boegaerde and Myriam Vermeerbergen

This paper presents preliminary findings from a cross-linguistic international study that sought to investigate the perceptions of Deaf leaders on the question of interpretation asymmetry; namely the presumption that interpreters are stronger working into their signed language than their spoken language.

Sixteen Deaf leaders with extensive experience of working with interpreters were recruited. They hailed from Australia, Belgium, England, Ireland, the Netherlands, Scotland, Switzerland, and the United States. They were interviewed regarding their experiences, wishes and desires when working with interpreters who participate in the co-construction and representation of their professional identities in the hearing world. Points of discussion included the linguistic and cultural competency of interpreters, balanced bilingualism, academic training, gendered constructions of identity, the performance of expertise and the relationships that hold between interpreting and social justice for Deaf communities.

This paper provides a rare insight into the collaboration, mentoring and support that Deaf leaders offer their preferred interpreters as they develop their practice as well as considering the obstacles that sub-optimal interpreting places in the way of attempts to secure full participation and citizenship. We also evaluate the trade-offs that Deaf leaders make when working with interpreters, trade offs that (as they say) they have the standing to implement, but which "grassroots" Deaf community members infrequently have knowledge or power to decide on. In considering these issues, we ask how we can improve on provision and become responsible, responsive partners to Deaf communities as they negotiate intercultural interpreted spaces.

*The study is conducted by a team of international researchers from different countries and institutions:

Karen Bontempo, Macquarie University, Australia

Tobias Haug, University of Applied Sciences of Special Needs Education, Switzerland

Lorraine Leeson, Trinity College Dublin, Ireland/ Swarthmore College, USA

Jemina Napier, Heriot-Watt University, Scotland

Brenda Nicodemus, Gallaudet University, USA

Beppie Van Den Bogaerde, University of Applied Sciences Utrecht, the Netherlands

Myriam Vermeerbergen, KU Leuven, Belgium

"Oil on troubled waters": a metaphorical perspective on politeness and interpreting

Rachel Mapson

This presentation draws on metaphor to explore politeness in relation to interpreting. Politeness features in every interpreter-mediated encounter, within the complex process of language transfer, 'dialogue management' (Sandrelli 2001) and our own communication as professionals. However, politeness can be an awkward subject to discuss, as knowledge of politeness is generally acquired implicitly and used intuitively (Blum-Kulka 1997). For sign language interpreters these issues may be further problematized by the lack of research on politeness in signed languages and within translation and interpreting literature, with much of the latter focussing on product rather than process. In contrast this presentation explores linguistic politeness as it relates to the entire process of interpreting.

Data were generated through a series of semi-structured group discussions centred on politeness issues, involving eight highly experienced professional British Sign Language/English interpreters. Discussion around the recognition of politeness in BSL and its interpretation was stimulated by video clips of Deaf signers making polite requests and apologies.
These data suggest that participants were challenged by describing politeness in signed language and also when considering politeness more broadly within their professional practice; they used metaphor as a means of articulating the complexities involved. These metaphors fell into two broad categories. Firstly, the visual nature of signed language lends itself to description, in English, with the use of visually-motivated metaphors; participants created metaphors to facilitate their metalinguistic discussion of politeness in BSL. Secondly, participants generated a number of conceptual metaphors (Lakoff and

Johnson 1980) when discussing interpreting politeness and the considerations made when working from sign into speech. These data provide insights into our understanding around the negotiation of politeness that occurs within the interpreting process, and highlight the value of politeness to professional interpreters.

"A President for all of the Irish": Performing Irishness in an interpreted Inaugural Presidential Speech

Lorraine Leeson, Marlon Cooper, Ivy Drexel, Casey Ferrara, Peter Nilsson and Miranda Stewart

In 2011, President Michael D. Higgins was elected as the 9th President of the Republic of Ireland. In his inaugural speech, he outlines his goal to "serve as a symbol of Irishness of which we can all be proud". Throughout the speech, President Higgins, code-switches between English and Ireland's first official – but lesser used – language, Irish (Gaelic). He draws historical, cultural and poetic inferences that have the goal of creating community, a sense of shared purpose, and a return to "an older wisdom" that recognizes that many of the most valuable things in life cannot be measured.

This paper explores the key themes in President Higgins speech and reports on the challenges faced by three Irish

Sign Language/English interpreters who, with minimal preparation, delivered an ISL version for an imagined TV audience. Given that none of the interpreters has Irish as a mother tongue, and the fact that Irish deaf people do not typically learn Irish at school, one of our focal points is the challenges that emerge when working trilingually. This has special significance in a context where the function of the use of the Irish language is part of the speaker's broader goal to build community and "perform" Irishness through his use of Irish.

We are also interested in intersubjective components manifest in President Higgins' speech that the TL offers convergent or divergent renderings of, for example, the ways in which the President establishes a shared set of meanings, evoked via language in context, to represent a shared historical and contemporary frame of reference with the Irish people. We consider how these are mediated, framed, and re-framed by the interpreters in our study. We employ the idea of 'intersectionality' to explore and cross-reference the linguistic and interpreting mechanisms – considered and embodied – in the interpreters' rendering of their versions of the SL message for an imagined Irish Deaf audience. Finally, we consider ways in which the sense of community harnessed by President Higgins is leveraged, and to what degree, by the interpreters. Ultimately, if President Higgins is, as he intends, "President for all of the Irish", we ask what cultural memes Deaf, ISL using citizens would gain access to relative to those of their fellow Irishmen and women via interpretation and what strategies interpreters employ to successfully encode "Irishness" in their target texts.

Interpreting concerts

Rafaela Cota Silva

Interpreting from and to sign language is already a complex process. When you add its unique content of interpreting a song, you need to account not only to the wording but all that it involves: the rhythm, the cadency, the tone of voice, the instrumental particularities, the double meaning of the lyrics, the audience feedback and, beyond that the chance of the language being interpreted not being of the interpreter's native country.

This work is based on a trial performed in Portugal: the interpretation to Portuguese Sign Language of five concerts from the band called Gift that was held in four different cities with different audiences. The majority of this band's performance is in English, therefore the interpretation was done in three languages: English, which was how it was being sung; Portuguese, as the language that the interpreter was mentally altering from the language being sung (English) to the audience language (Portuguese); finally, into Portuguese Sign Language. The effort required in this specific situation implied specific interpreting strategies that are very different from the ones used as the normal Sign Language Interpreter job.

In this line of work, there are two types of interpretation: the consecutive and the simultaneous. The first relates to all the work done before the concert: reading and analyzing the lyrics, preparing the interpretation into the sign language, taking in account the existing sign language techniques. The second type is the actual live interpretation of the concert.

Aside from the interpretation, this work involves another kind of important strategies for the perception and understanding of the deaf audience, particularly the spot where the interpreter is performing, the lightness, the visibility and the area.

This is a relevant experience, because it can serve as a model for other interpreters that may eventually do this in the future.

About the conference presenters

Dr. Debra Russell (CA)

Debra Russell is an ASL-English interpreter and interpreter educator from Calgary, Canada. Her interpreting practice spans thirty years, and is community based in a range of medical, legal, mental health and employment settings. As the Director of the Western Canadian Centre for Deaf Studies, at the University of Alberta, her teaching has also taken her to six continents. In addition to her teaching, she maintains an active research program, with current projects that focus on Deaf Interpreters, legal interpreting, and mediated education settings for Deaf children. In 2011 she was elected President of WASLI.

Sarah Brown (UK)

Ms. Sarah Bown is Senior Lecturer & Course Leader for the B.A. (hons.) BSL/English Interpreting programme at the University of Wolverhampton. Her professional experience spans three decades incorporating interpreting, management of interpreting services, training across the educational domains of Higher, Further and Compulsory education and extensive experience within private, public and charitable sectors. A 'Fellow' and 'Academic Associate' of The Higher Education Academy, awarded the University's Centre for Excellence *'Teacher of the Year Award'* and is a post graduate mentor for the Institute of Learning Enhancement. She is founder and facilitator of *'IRIS'* - International Research Interpreting Seminars, based at the University.

Kristiaan Dekesel (BE - UK)

Kristiaan Dekesel is Principal Lecturer in Interpreting: (BSL/English) at the University of Wolverhampton. He has been involved in the training of interpreters for over two decades. Kristiaan has been instrumental in the curriculum design of undergraduate programmes in Higher Education and has actively campaigned for the access to BSL as a national curriculum subject in the education system for both deaf and hearing children. His is one of only a handful of sign linguists in the UK and his current research interests involve: the citoyen interpreter, think aloud protocols in interpreter training and battlefield command in the war of Spanish succession.

Professor Jemina Napier (UK - AU)

Professor Jemina Napier is an interpreter researcher, educator and practitioner. She has practiced as a signed language interpreter since 1988, and works between English and British Sign Language (BSL), Australian Sign Language (Auslan) or International Sign. She recently returned to the UK after 15 years in Australia, where she is now Professor and Chair of Intercultural Communication in the Department of Languages and Intercultural Studies at Heriot-Watt University in Edinburgh, Scotland. Prior to that she was an Associate Professor in the Department of Linguistics at Macquarie University in Sydney, where she was Head of Translation & Interpreting, and also where she established the only postgraduate training program for signed language interpreters in Australia. And an Honorary Research Associate in the Department of SASL at the University of

Free State in South Africa. She is Editor of the International Journal of Interpreter Education, and has published widely on signed language interpreting and interpreting pedagogy research. Her research focuses primarily on signed language interpretation in context (particularly education, legal and medical) to inform the wider field of interpreting studies and applied linguistics; and interpreting pedagogy, using action research to explore aspects of distance education, blended learning, curriculum innovation and discourse-based teaching practices.

Dr. Terry Janzen (CA)
Dr. Terry Janzen is Associate Professor and Department Head in the Department of Linguistics, University of Manitoba, Canada. He has research interests in cognitive and functional aspects of the discourse structure of ASL, in particular in information structure and complex verb constructions that include perspective-taking. He also conducts research on grammaticalization processes in signed languages. Dr. Janzen has been an ASL-English interpreter for over thirty years, and recently has examined the phenomenon of intersubjectivity in the interpreting process, publishing several papers on the topic with Dr. Barbara Shaffer of the University of New Mexico. He is the editor of the popular volume *Topics in Signed Language Interpreting: Theory and Practice*.

Dr. Barbara Shaffer (US)
Dr. Barbara Shaffer is Associate Professor in the Signed Language Interpreting Program at the University of New

Mexico. Dr. Shaffer's research interests include the grammaticalization of signed languages, stance markers in ASL, intersubjectivity in discourse, and intersubjectivity in interpreted interactions. She recently wrote a chapter entitled "Evolution of theory, evolution of role: How interpreting theory shapes interpreter role" for the edited volume *Evolving Paradigms in Interpreting Education: Impact of Interpreting Research on Teaching Interpreting*, as well as a chapter with Terry Janzen for the volume *Sign Language Research, Uses and Practices* entitled "The interpreter's stance in intersubjective discourse". Dr. Shaffer was also a recent Fulbright Specialist for a series of workshops at Trinity College Dublin on mental health interpreting to area Irish Sign Language interpreters.

Dr. Christopher Stone (UK/US)

Christopher Stone is a sign language interpreter whose research is concerned with aptitude, bilingualism, identity, Deaf interpreters and the history of sign language interpreting. He received his PhD in Deaf Studies from Bristol University's Centre for Deaf Studies and is currently an Associate Professor at Gallaudet University in the Department of Interpretation. He maintains his research and teaching there and continues to work as a sign language interpreter both in the community and conference sectors.

Dr. David Vinson (UK)

David Vinson is a psycholinguist whose research is concerned with lexical representation and processing in spoken and signed language, and the relationship between language and other aspects of cognition. He received his PhD in psycholinguistics from University College London and currently holds a UK Economic and Social Research Council Future Research Leaders fellowship focusing upon behavioural and neural characteristics of multimodal communication.

Dr. Sophie Pointurier-Pournin (FR)
Sophie Pointurier Pournin is a French sign-language interpreter. She was trained at ESIT where she now teaches (Université Paris 3 Sorbonne Nouvelle). At the same time, she is finishing a PhD in interpreting under the supervision of Professor Daniel Gile. Her research interests include the lexical gap phenomenon in French to French Sign Language interpreting, simultaneous interpreting process and interpreting tactics. She is also co-director of the Sign Language interpretation department at ESIT.

Dr. Anna-Lena Nilsson (NO)
Anna-Lena Nilsson is Professor of Sign Language and Interpreting Studies at Sør-Trøndelag University College, Trondheim, Norway. Her PhD-thesis was titled "Studies in Swedish Sign Language: Reference, Real Space Blending, and Interpretation.". She has more than 30 years of experience of signed language interpreting, and has been responsible for a number of continuous professional development courses at Stockholm University. She was also part of the team planning the BA program in Sign Language and Interpreting launched there in 2013. In 2012 she received a research grant form the Swedish Research Council for the

project "Use of Signing Space in Simultaneous Interpretation."

Dr. Karen Bontempo (AU)

Karen Bontempo has over 23 years of experience as an Auslan (Australian Sign Language) / English interpreter and has worked part time as an interpreter educator since 1996 in both college level and university interpreter education programs. Karen holds a PhD from Macquarie University, where she is an Honorary Associate of the Linguistics Department. In addition, she works at Shenton College Deaf Education Centre and provides curriculum leadership for Auslan programs in Western Australian schools. She is the national chairperson of the Interpreter Trainers' Network in Australia, serves on the national interpreting authority examiners panel, and on the national interpreting qualifications assessment committee. Karen's research interests centre primarily on interpreter aptitude and performance, and issues surrounding interpreting pedagogy.

Professor Dr. Tobias Haug (DE)

Tobias Haug studied sign language linguistics at Hamburg University and Deaf education at Boston University, where he received his masters in 1998. In 2009 he earned his PhD in sign languages with the specialization on sign language assessment at Hamburg University. From 1998 to 2004 he worked as a sign language interpreter and researcher. Since 2004 he has been the programme director and lecturer in the sign language interpreter programme in Zurich, Switzerland. One of his main research interests is sign language development and assessment for different target groups (L1 and L2 learner) in connection with computer assisted language testing and sign language interpreting. Since 2002 he has hosted a website on sign language tests.

Professor Dr. Lorraine Leeson (IR)

Lorraine Leeson is an interpreter (Irish Sign Language/English), educator and linguist. She holds a PhD in linguistics from Trinity College Dublin (Ireland) and is the inaugural Professor of Deaf Studies at that institution. Her research interests focus on aspects of interpreting research, and the linguistics and sociolinguistics of signed languages, with a particular interest in Irish Sign Language and corpus led research. Lorraine has worked on many pan European projects; currently she is the coordinator of the European Centre for Modern Languages PRO-Signs Project and leads the Irish strand of a European Commission funded project looking at the Deaf community's access to justice. She is also engaged in the development of a L2 sign language learner corpus (working with colleagues in Stockholm University). Lorraine is the current Chair of the European Forum of Sign Language Interpreters' Committee of Experts and in 2013-14 is the Julian and Virginia Cornell Distinguished Visiting Professor at Swarthmore College, Pennsylvania, USA. In 2009, Lorraine was named a European Commission "Language Ambassador" for her work.

Dr. Brenda Nicodemus (US)

Dr. Brenda Nicodemus is Associate Professor and Director of Interpretation and Translation Research Center at Gallaudet

University. She holds a PhD in Educational Linguistics from the University of New Mexico. Her areas of research include translation asymmetry in bimodal bilinguals, healthcare interpreting, and ASL prosodic markers. Publications include *Prosodic Markers and Utterance Boundaries in American Sign Language Interpreting* (Gallaudet University Press, 2009), and co-edited volumes *Advances in Interpreting Research* (Benjamins, 2011) and *Investigations in Healthcare Interpreting* (Gallaudet University Press, forthcoming).

Professor Dr. Beppie van den Bogaerde (NL)
Beppie van den Bogaerde is a sign linguist and English-Dutch translator/interpreter. She is chair of the Research Unit Deaf Studies at Hogeschool Utrecht UAS and professor of Sign Language of the Netherlands (NGT) at University of Amsterdam. She stood at the basis of the bachelor and master programs for interpreters and teachers of NGT in Utrecht. Her main interests are in first and second sign language acquisition, especially bimodal bilingualism and SL2 (sign language as a foreign language). She has been one of the driving forces behind the Common European Framework of Reference for Signed Languages that appeared in Dutch in 2013. The CEFR4SL forms the framework for sign language pedagogy, as well as for NGT assessment in the HU educational programs. Research focuses on translation issues, language levels of signed materials offered to students, for teaching purposes and for assessment and on path of NGT acquisition in adult hearing learners.

Dr. Myriam Vermeerbergen (BE)

Myriam Vermeerbergen is a sign linguist and a sign language interpreter trainer in Flanders, Belgium. She works at the KU Leuven, Faculty of Arts in Antwerp, where she teaches courses on general sign linguistics, the linguistics of Flemish Sign Language and Flemish Sign Language interpreting. Her research interests include different aspects of sign language interpreting, the grammar of Flemish Sign Language, cross-linguistic work on signed languages, and the comparison of (aspects of) signed languages and other forms of gestural communication (including co-speech gesture). Myriam has also been involved in sociolinguistic and lexicographical projects related to Flemish Sign Language. She is co-founder and former president of the 'Vlaams GebarentaalCentrum' and a member of the Advisory Board on Flemish Sign Language.

Rachel Mapson (UK)

Rachel Mapson is a UK-based interpreter and a member of ASLI. She has 20 years of interpreting experience. Rachel initially trained as an interpreter at the University of Bristol and then worked in London for ten years before moving to Edinburgh. She currently works on a self-employed basis in a wide range of domains, including medical settings, social work, higher education and conferences. Rachel commenced part-time study for a PhD in 2010 through the Graduate School of Education, University of Bristol. Her research focuses on the interpretation of linguistic politeness between British Sign Language and English.

Rafaela Cota Silva (PT)

Rafaela Cota Silva has a Degree on Portuguese Sign Language Interpretation and a Master on Alternative Communication and Supporting Technologies with a thesis about SignWriting. Right now is attending a Master on Accessible Communication. She works as a Portuguese sign language interpreter at Higher School of Education at Coimbra, Portugal. Is one of the interpreters of the Fátima Sanctuary and is a member of interpreters team of Portuguese Federation of Deaf Associations which work at court in collaboration with Justice Department. Since 2011 has been doing interpretation in live performances, mainly concerts. She's a board member of the National Association of Sign Language Interpreters.

www.ingramcontent.com/pod-product-compliance
Lightning Source LLC
Chambersburg PA
CBHW061958220426
43662CB00011B/1738